KITCHEN TABLE

100 Foolproof Suppers

my KITCHEN TABLE gives you a wealth of recipes from your favourite chefs. Whether you want a quick weekday supper, sumptuous weekend feast or food for friends and family, let the My Kitchen Table experts bring their favourite dishes to your home.

To find out more about our exciting **my** recipe App, get exclusive recipes, read our blog or subscribe to our newsletter, visit our site at www.mykitchentable.co.uk

Throughout this book, when you see **my** visit the website for practical videos, tips and hints from the My Kitchen Table team.

KITCHEN
TABLE

100 Foolproof Suppers
GIZZI ERSKINE

www.mykitchentable.co.uk

Welcome to  KITCHEN TABLE

Face the kitchen with more gusto, and learn to
develop your cooking confidence, with this collection
of **100 of my favourite supper recipes** that are
fast, foolproof and full of flavour!

Contents

Mexican Chicken Tortilla Soup

If you go to any street market in Mexico they will be selling a variation on this soup. It is actually a cleansing broth with a hot-and-sour note, filled with chunky chicken and sweetcorn and topped with creamy avocado and swirls of crisp tortilla. The tortillas act like croutons and stay crisp on top but soak up all the lip-smacking juices underneath.

Step one Heat 2 tablespoons of the oil in a large pan over a low heat. Add the onions and fry for 10 minutes, or until they have softened and started to turn a golden colour. For the last minute, add the garlic and chillies. Throw in the tomatoes, then pour over the stock. Add the sweetcorn and chicken breasts and simmer gently for 15 minutes.

Step two Remove the chicken breast and set aside. Cook the soup for a further 10 minutes. Season to taste.

Step three Shred the chicken and return it to the soup, along with any juices. Heat the remaining tablespoon of oil in a frying pan over a medium heat. Toss in the tortilla strips and fry for 3 minutes, or until crisp and golden. Ladle the soup into bowls and top with a sprinkling of tortillas, some avocado and coriander.

For an even speedier soup, why not add tortilla chips, unfried, instead of fried flour tortillas?

Serves 4

3 tbsp olive oil

2 onions, finely chopped

4 garlic cloves, finely chopped

2 red or green chillies, seeded and chopped

3 ripe tomatoes, chopped

900ml (1½ pints) chicken stock

275g (10oz) tin sweetcorn, drained

2 chicken breasts, skinned

sea salt and freshly ground black pepper

for the topping

2 medium (20cm/8in) flour tortillas, cut in half then thinly sliced

1 avocado, chopped

a handful of fresh coriander leaves, to serve

Posh Tomato Soup with Cappelletti

Smoked tomatoes may not be widely available, but you should be able to find them at farmers' markets. If you can't, use the same quantity of sunblush tomatoes mixed with 1 teaspoon of smoked paprika. Cappelletti are simply tiny filled pasta (I love the ones filled with goats' cheese), similar to tortellini, but if you can't find them use any small stuffed pasta you like.

Serves 4 as a starter or 2 as a main course

3 red peppers, seeded and halved

5 vine tomatoes, halved

2 tbsp olive oil

1 onion, finely chopped

3 garlic cloves, finely chopped

100g (4oz) oak-smoked tomatoes, or the same quantity sunblush tomatoes mixed with 1 tsp smoked paprika

200ml (6fl oz) vegetable stock

3 fresh basil sprigs

100g (4oz) cappelletti of your choice

pesto, to drizzle

grated Parmesan cheese, to serve

sea salt and freshly ground black pepper

Step one Preheat the oven to 200°C/400°F/gas 6. Lay the pepper halves, cut-side up, on a baking sheet and top with the vine tomato halves. Drizzle with 1 tablespoon of olive oil and season with salt and pepper. Roast for 25 minutes, or until the peppers and tomatoes are starting to blacken and have softened.

Step two Meanwhile, heat the remaining tablespoon of oil in a pan over a fairly low heat. Throw in the onions and fry for 10 minutes, so that they become really softened and start to caramelise and sweeten. For the last minute of the cooking time, add the garlic.

Step three When the peppers and tomatoes are done, put them into a blender with the onions, garlic, smoked tomatoes, vegetable stock and basil sprigs. Process for 2 minutes, until smooth, then return the soup to the pan. For a really smooth consistency, you can sieve it from the blender into the pan. Reheat very gently over a low heat.

Step four Meanwhile, bring a pan of salted water to the boil. Add the cappelletti and boil for 1–2 minutes, then drain. Ladle the soup into bowls and top each serving with some of the cappelletti, a drizzle of pesto and a grating of Parmesan.

Gazpacho with King Prawns and Quail's Eggs

A gazpacho has all the components of a salad, even down to the dressing and the croutons. On its own it's brilliant – with prawns and quail's eggs it turns into a dish that will wow anyone.

Step one Place all the ingredients for the gazpacho in a mixing bowl and toss as if you're making a salad. Place half this mixture in a blender and blitz for 1 minute, or until smooth. Push the soup through a fine sieve into another mixing bowl. Repeat with the other half of the 'salad'. Check the seasoning and cool in the fridge for an hour. (You can eat the soup immediately but it does benefit from a bit of chilling time.)

Step two While the soup is chilling, hard-boil your quail's eggs in a pan of boiling water for 7 minutes, and prepare the topping ingredients. When you're ready to serve the gazpacho, ladle it into bowls. Top each bowl with some of the chopped vegetables, 3 king prawns and 3 halves of quail's egg, and drizzle with a little olive oil.

Serves 4

1kg (2lb) vine-ripened tomatoes, skinned

½ cucumber, peeled and chopped

1 red pepper, seeded and chopped

1 red chilli

3 garlic cloves, peeled

100g (4oz) white bread, crusts removed, soaked in water

1 fresh basil sprig

100ml (4fl oz) extra virgin olive oil, plus extra for drizzling

2 tbsp sherry vinegar

1 tsp golden caster sugar

sea salt and freshly ground black pepper

to serve

6 hard-boiled quail's eggs, shelled and halved

1 tomato, seeded and chopped

¼ cucumber, seeded and chopped

¼ red pepper, seeded and chopped

12 cooked king prawns, peeled

Have you made this recipe? Tell us what you think at www.mykitchentable.co.uk/blog

Chicken Satay Noodle Soup

I am an Asian food freak, and I make something Asian pretty much on a daily basis. It's so fast to cook and fresh.

Serves 4

4 boneless chicken thighs

1 tsp ground coriander

½ tsp turmeric

½ tsp dried chillies

1 tsp sea salt

1 tbsp olive oil

400g (14oz) tin coconut milk

400ml (14fl oz) chicken stock

2½ tbsp yellow curry paste

1 tbsp peanut butter

2 tbsp Thai fish sauce

2 tbsp brown sugar

juice of ½ lemon

1 tbsp chilli oil

250g (9oz) rice noodles

sea salt and freshly ground black pepper

to serve

a small bunch each fresh coriander and mint, chopped

¼ cucumber, sliced

2 spring onions, sliced

2 handfuls of beansprouts

1 red chilli, sliced

a large handful of roasted peanuts or cashews

Step one Rub the chicken thighs with the ground coriander, turmeric, dried chillies and salt. Heat the oil in a frying pan over a lowish heat, add the thighs, skin-side down, and fry for 10 minutes, or until the skin is crispy. Turn them over and cook for a further 6 minutes. Set the pan aside and let the chicken rest, skin-side up, in the pan.

Step two Put the coconut milk, stock, curry paste, peanut butter, fish sauce, brown sugar, lemon juice and chilli oil into a pan over a low heat and stir until the sugar has dissolved. Increase the heat, bring to the boil, and cook for 5 minutes. Season to taste.

Step three Cook the rice noodles according to the packet instructions and divide between 4 bowls. Ladle the soup into the bowls, then top each serving with some coriander, mint, cucumber, spring onions, beansprouts, chilli and chopped nuts. Slice the chicken thighs and distribute between the bowls. Serve piping hot.

Chinese Chicken & Mushroom Soup with Sesame Prawn Toast Croutons

You don't get much more British than chicken and mushroom soup unless, of course, you cook the chicken and mushrooms with an aromatic broth of ginger, soy and sesame and add heat in the form of red chillies.

Step one Add 1 tablespoon of olive oil to a large, heavy-based pan over a medium heat. Peel and slice the ginger and stir-fry with the garlic for 1 minute, or until they start to take on some colour. Throw in the chicken and mushrooms and stir-fry for a further 5 minutes, or until lightly golden.

Step two Cover with the hot stock, then reduce the heat to low. Add the soy sauce and sesame oil. In a separate small bowl mix 5 tablespoons of the hot liquid with the cornflour. This will become paste-like, so you may need to add more stock to make it a little runny. Pour it into the soup, stirring as you go. After a few minutes, the soup will begin to thicken. Leave it to simmer away for 10 minutes.

Step three Meanwhile, make the sesame prawn toast croutons. Place the prawns, egg white, cream, a generous squeeze of lemon juice and a pinch of nutmeg in a food-processor, add a pinch of salt and pulse every so often until you have a chunky purée. Spread this in a thick layer on the slices of bread, then coat the purée with the sesame seeds.

Step four Add the remaining olive oil to a frying pan over a medium heat. Place the toast croutons, sesame-seed-side down in the oil and fry for a few minutes on each side, or until the sesame seeds are toasted and the bread is crisp and golden. Drain on kitchen paper.

Step five Add the spring onions to the soup for the last minute of cooking, then ladle into bowls. Top with the sliced chillies and serve each bowl with 2 sesame prawn toast croutons.

Serves 4

4 tbsp olive oil

5cm (2in) piece fresh root ginger

3 garlic cloves, crushed

2 boneless chicken breasts, each cut into 15–20 chunks

20 shiitake mushrooms, halved or quartered

1 litre (1¾ pints) hot chicken stock

1 tbsp soy sauce

1 tsp sesame oil

1 rounded tbsp cornflour

for the toast croutons

8 raw king prawns, peeled

1 egg white

1 tbsp double cream

lemon juice

a pinch of nutmeg

1 small baguette, cut diagonally into 8 slices

sesame seeds

sea salt

to serve

4 spring onions, chopped

1 red chilli, seeded and thinly sliced

15

Smoked Ham and Piccalilli Salad

I love piccalilli and really wanted to find a way to put it into a salad, but, alas, it doesn't seem to work – it's all a bit too gungy. So instead I decided to make a salad with crunchy peppery vegetables and drizzle it with a fantastic, fragrant, light, bright yellow dressing.

Serves 4

½ cauliflower, broken into florets

30 green beans, trimmed

2 radishes, thinly sliced

2 carrots, thinly sliced

¼ red onion, thinly sliced

2 gherkins, thinly sliced

1 head chicory

1 head Little Gem lettuce

200g (7oz) smoked ham, preferably torn from a ham hock, or thickly sliced ham, torn into pieces

for the dressing

1 tsp English mustard powder

½ tsp ground turmeric

a pinch of allspice

a grating of nutmeg

½ garlic clove, grated

½ tsp sugar

2 tbsp cider vinegar

3 tbsp extra virgin olive oil

sea salt and freshly ground black pepper

Step one Bring a pan of salted water to the boil and throw in the cauliflower and beans. Boil for 2 minutes, then drain and plunge immediately into iced water to cool and stop the cooking process. When they have cooled, drain and place in a mixing bowl with the radishes, carrots, onion and gherkins.

Step two To make the dressing, place all the ingredients in a clean jam jar, screw the lid on tightly and shake like crazy for 30 seconds. Pour half the dressing over the crunchy vegetables and mix thoroughly.

Step three Separate, wash and dry the leaves of the chicory and Little Gem lettuce. Place on a large plate and drizzle with the rest of the dressing. Top with the crunchy vegetables and torn ham and serve immediately.

Sticky Thai Chicken and Mango Salad

If we were in Thailand we would be eating this salad with firm, under-ripe, mouth-puckering green mangoes, but the crispy chicken also sings alongside creamy, juicy ripe ones. A pomelo, which is like a giant grapefruit, would make a fantastic alternative to mango in this salad. Simply swap the mango for half a pomelo, peeled and segmented. This salad's sweet, it's sticky, it's sour, it's hot, it's refreshing. So, although it may not be completely authentic, there is no denying it's jolly good.

Step one Heat the oil in a frying pan over a medium to low heat. Rub the chicken thighs with salt and pepper and lay them skin-side down in the pan. Cook for 6–8 minutes, then turn them over and repeat on the other side until they are cooked through and the skin is crisp and golden. Remove the chicken from the pan and set aside while you make the glaze.

Step two Add the fish sauce to the pan, along with the sugar, lime juice, ginger and chilli, and stir until the sugar has dissolved. Let the sauce bubble for a few seconds, then return the chicken thighs to the pan and coat them in the sauce. Remove the pan from the heat and set aside.

Step three To make the salad, heat the oil in a smaller frying pan over a medium to high heat and add two-thirds of the shallots. Stir-fry them for 5 minutes or until crisp and golden, then turn them out on to a sheet of kitchen paper to cool and drain.

Step four Peel the mango, then slice each of the cheeks off. Slice the mango flesh into long, thin slivers and put them into a bowl with the remaining uncooked shallots, chilli strips and herbs. In a smaller bowl, mix together the lime juice, fish sauce and sugar, and pour over the salad. Toss the salad and divide it between 4 plates.

Step five Slice the chicken and put a few slices on each plate. Sprinkle with some of the crispy shallots, then drizzle the remaining sauce in the pan over the chicken and serve.

Serves 4

1 tbsp olive oil

4 boneless chicken thighs, skin left on

3 tbsp Thai fish sauce

3 tbsp golden caster sugar

1 tbsp lime juice

3cm (1¼ in) piece fresh root ginger, peeled and grated

1 red Thai chilli, chopped

sea salt and freshly ground black pepper

for the salad

2 tbsp olive oil

8 banana shallots, sliced

1 ripe but firm mango

2 red chillies, seeded and cut into thin strips

a small bunch fresh coriander leaves

a small bunch fresh mint leaves

juice of 2 limes

2 tbsp Thai fish sauce

1 tsp caster sugar

19

Spiced Cauliflower Soup with Cauliflower Bhajis

Cauliflower bhajis really give you something to get your teeth into.

Serves 6

2 tbsp vegetable oil

1 large onion, chopped

2 tsp ground cumin

1 tsp ground coriander

1 medium-sized cauliflower, cut into florets

1.25 litres (2¼ pints) chicken or vegetable stock

100ml (4fl oz) double cream

sea salt and freshly ground black pepper

for the bhajis

100g (4oz) gram or plain flour

1 tsp ground cumin

½ tsp ground coriander

¼ tsp ground turmeric

1 egg

150ml (¼ pint) ice-cold fizzy water

vegetable oil, for deep-frying

200g (7oz) cauliflower, cut into small florets

a small bunch fresh coriander, stems discarded, leaves chopped, to garnish

Step one First make the soup. Heat the oil in a large pan on a low heat and add the chopped onion. Sweat the onion for 5 minutes or until softened. Add the ground cumin and coriander and mix together then add the cauliflower and stir to coat. Pour over the chicken or vegetable stock. Bring to the boil, then reduce the heat and simmer for 10 minutes or until the cauliflower is quite tender.

Step two Pour the soup into a blender and whizz until smooth. Pour it back into the pan, add the cream and heat gently. Season with lots of salt and pepper.

Step three To make the bhajis, mix together all of the ingredients (apart from the cauliflower and oil to make a batter) and season with ½ teaspoon of salt and lots of black pepper. Do not over-mix it as this will make the batter tough. Heat the oil until a piece of bread dropped into it browns in 30 seconds. Coat the cauliflower pieces in the batter, then carefully drop them into the hot oil and fry until golden brown. Drain on some kitchen paper. Serve scattered over the soup, along with some chopped coriander.

Mixed Vegetables with Chilli Honey Butter

Mixed vegetables are one of many things you can use this honey butter for, and I would recommend always having some in the fridge so you can throw a quick meal together. It's also spectacular with prawns, steak or corn on the cob, and just as terrific on toast! In this recipe I'm using it with a vibrant collection of mixed veggies. This is a staple in our household, either for a quick weeknight supper with some grilled meat or fish, or as part of your Sunday roast. I challenge you not to become addicted!

Step one Mix all the chilli honey butter ingredients together in a bowl and mash well with the back of a fork. Lay out a double 30cm (12in) piece of clingfilm on a work surface and pile the mashed butter into the centre. Roll the clingfilm over the butter and squeeze into a sausage shape. Twist the ends as tightly as possible in opposite directions so you have a neatly sealed roll of chilli honey butter. Chill for at least an hour.

Step two When you're ready to use the butter, place a large sauté pan over a low to medium heat. Remove the chilli butter from the fridge, peel back the cling film and cut off a couple of slices. Add them to the sauté pan to melt slowly. Reseal the rest of the butter and return it to the fridge. Tip in the prepared vegetables and sauté over a medium heat for 5 minutes, or until softened. Sprinkle over the parsley and serve piping hot.

Serves 4

1 courgette, trimmed, halved and sliced lengthways

100g (4oz) long, thin baby carrots, or 1 large carrot, halved and sliced lengthways

100g (4oz) broccoli florets

100g (4oz) baby leeks, halved lengthways

100g (4oz) green beans, trimmed

1 tbsp chopped fresh parsley

for the chilli honey butter

125g (4½ oz) butter, at room temperature

1½ tbsp honey

1 tsp cayenne pepper

a pinch of salt

Purple Sprouting Broccoli with Stilton Sauce

Purple sprouting broccoli is terribly fashionable now, but I know quite a few people still don't really know how to work with it. I remember getting hooked on it after seeing Hugh Fearnley-Whittingstall serve it with a blue cheese sauce. Here's my interpretation.

Serves 4

25g (1oz) butter

25g (1oz) plain flour

300ml (½ pint) milk

150g (5oz) Stilton cheese, crumbled

450g (1lb) purple sprouting broccoli, leaves and stalks, cut into 10cm (4in) lengths

sea salt and freshly ground black pepper

Step one Melt the butter in a small saucepan over a low heat. Add the flour and stir over a low heat for 1 minute, until the mixture foams. Remove from the heat and gradually stir in the milk. The sauce will thicken almost straight away, but the more milk you add the thinner it will get. If you don't add the milk very slowly it will become lumpy.

Step two Put the pan back on the heat and stir until gently boiling. Boil for 2 minutes, continuing to stir to prevent it catching on the bottom of the pan. Add the cheese and stir until melted. Season with salt and pepper.

Step three Bring a large pan of salted water to the boil. Chuck in the broccoli and boil for 3–4 minutes, or until tender but still retaining some bite. Drain, then transfer to a serving dish. Pour over the Stilton sauce and serve.

Red Cabbage with Apples and Sultanas

There are not many side dishes that stand out as much as, if not more than, the meat or fish you might be serving them with. But a good red cabbage dish that's a little bit sweet and a little bit sour rocks! My mum's part Polish, and hers is the best I've had. It needs a while to cook, and those who are not big fans of sultanas can simply leave them out. At home we eat this with pork chops, shepherd's pie or venison.

Step one Add the olive oil to a large wok or pan over a low to medium heat. Fry the onions gently for 8 minutes, or until they have softened and started to turn golden.

Step two Add the cabbage and stir-fry for a further 5 minutes. Add the vinegar, water and sugar and stir until the sugar has dissolved, then cover and simmer gently for 20 minutes.

Step three Add the apples and sultanas and cook for a further 20 minutes. You may need to check the water level at this stage. You don't want it too dry, but it shouldn't be too wet either. When you move the cabbage away with a spoon it should slowly leave a trail of lightly syrupy liquid. Season with salt and pepper and serve.

For a more savoury version of the dish, add some crisp pancetta at the beginning of cooking.

Serves 4

2 tbsp olive oil

2 red onions, thinly sliced

½ large red cabbage (or 1 small one), cored and thinly sliced

150ml (¼ pint) red wine vinegar

150ml (¼ pint) water

3 tbsp brown sugar

2 apples, any firm variety, peeled, cored and thinly sliced

50g (2oz) sultanas

sea salt and freshly ground black pepper

For a video masterclass on chopping vegetables, go to
www.mykitchentable.co.uk/videos/choppingvegetables

Root Vegetable Röstis

A perfect crisp rösti works brilliantly as a side dish, or you can eat it the traditional way as a main course. Röstis can be made with most things, and the addition of bacon, red peppers or spring onions brings them into a new dimension. I have made this one with a mixture of root vegetables, and it is dangerously good. Try it with a fried duck breast or even with a fried egg on top.

Makes 4

2 large carrots

2 large parsnips

3 tbsp olive oil

1 onion, finely chopped

2 large baking potatoes, peeled and grated

a few fresh thyme sprigs, leaves picked

sea salt and freshly ground black pepper

Step one Parboil the carrots and parsnips. Add 1 tablespoon of oil to a non-stick frying pan over a medium heat. Fry the onion for 5 minutes, until it has softened and started to go golden. Remove from the pan and leave to cool for 5 minutes on some kitchen paper. Meanwhile, grate the parboiled carrots and parsnips.

Step two Put the grated potato inside a clean tea towel and squeeze to remove excess water. Tip into a bowl and add the carrots, parsnips, onion and thyme leaves. Season really well and mix everything together. Divide into 4 portions and squeeze each one to make a cake-shape rösti.

Step three Preheat the oven to 200°C/400°F/gas 6. Add the remaining 2 tablespoons of oil to a non-stick frying pan over a medium heat. Place the röstis in the pan and cook for 6–8 minutes, or until golden brown and crisp underneath. Turn over and cook for a further 6–8 minutes, until golden on the other side. Pop onto a baking tray, bake for 5 minutes, and serve.

Try swapping the parsnips and carrots for another two large baking potatoes and making in the same way.

Filipino Fried Rice with Fried Eggs and Chorizo

I have just been food styling an Asian cookbook and while I consider myself quite an authority on Asian food, this simple but damn delicious breakfast dish really blew my mind. The recipe called for chorizo, which I suspect is because the cured spicy pork they use in the Philippines is a tad hard to get hold of. Using chorizo is great though, because frying an egg in the oil the chorizo leaves is a real treat and the spiciness complements everything perfectly. I wouldn't eat this just for breakfast, either; it's just as good as a light supper. Having never been to the Philippines I can't vouch for whether it's authentic, but it's a damn great dish. Plus, what a great way of using up leftover rice, and it's delicious served on its own or with meat and poultry dishes. If you don't have any leftover rice, cook 225g (8oz) the day before, using the absorption method, and keep it in the refrigerator.

Serves 4

2 tbsp groundnut oil

2–3 garlic cloves, chopped

450g (1lb) cooked long-grain rice

1–2 tbsp Filipino or Thai fish sauce

sea salt and freshly ground black pepper

to serve

2 tbsp groundnut oil

3 whole fresh chorizo sausages, sliced diagonally

4 eggs

4–6 tbsp coconut vinegar, or rice wine vinegar, for dipping (optional)

Step one Add the 2 tablespoons of oil to a wok or a heavy pan over a medium heat. Add the garlic, stirring it often, and fry until fragrant and golden. Toss in the rice, breaking up any lumps, then stir in the fish sauce. Season with salt, if needed, and black pepper, then turn off the heat and cover with a lid to keep warm.

Step two Just before serving, place 1 tablespoon of the oil in a heavy pan over a medium heat. Add the chorizo and fry until crispy on both sides. Remove from the pan and drain on kitchen paper. Meanwhile, in a separate pan, heat 1 tablespoon of oil over a low to medium heat and fry the eggs, making sure the yolk remains soft and runny.

Step three Tip the rice on to individual plates, place the egg on top, and arrange the fried chorizo around the edge. Serve warm with the coconut vinegar, if you like.

Butternut Squash, Pomegranate, Pine Nut, Feta and Mint Salad

Sticky roasted butternut squash with creamy feta, piquant pomegranate and a whole load of fresh mint is an exceptional salad on its own. However, if you really want to show off, pair it with a roasted leg of lamb and all of its scrummy juices.

Serves 4

½ large butternut squash, peeled and sliced into half moons 5mm (¼ in) thick

1 tbsp olive oil

a pinch of crushed chilli

a good pinch of coriander seed

a good pinch of cumin seeds

2 tbsp pine nuts, toasted

150g (5oz) feta cheese

1 pomegranate, seeds only (reserve any juice for the dressing)

a small bunch fresh mint, leaves picked

for the dressing

1 tbsp pomegranate molasses

½ tbsp lemon juice

a pinch of ground cinnamon

2 tbsp extra virgin olive oil

sea salt and freshly ground black pepper

Step one Heat the oven to 200°C/400°F/gas 6. Lay the prepared squash in a roasting tin and drizzle with the oil. Quickly bash together the chilli, coriander and spices in a pestle and mortar and season with salt and pepper. Sprinkle the mixture over the squash and toss to coat. Roast for 20–25 minutes, turning the pieces of squash over two–thirds of the way through.

Step two Pile the roast squash onto a serving plate or split between individual plates. Sprinkle over the pine nuts, crumble over the feta and scatter over the pomegranate seeds.

Step three Whisk together all the dressing ingredients, season to taste and drizzle over the salad. Finally scatter over the fresh mint leaves.

Bombay Potato Scotch Egg

Just when you think a Scotch egg couldn't get better, this one's vegetarian!

Step one Bring a pan of salted water to the boil. Cook five of the eggs for 6 minutes. Strain and leave to cool for 10 minutes in iced water, then peel.

Step two To make the spice mix, toast all the ingredients in a hot, dry frying pan until they begin to smoke lightly. Remove from the heat immediately and leave to cool for a few minutes. Place the spices in a spice grinder, coffee grinder or pestle and mortar, and blend to a fine powder.

Step three Finely chop the garlic and shallots, then peel and grate the ginger and seed and finely chop the chilli. Peel and chop the potatoes into 1 cm cubes. Heat the butter and rapeseed oil in a large heavy-based pan. Add the garlic, shallots, ginger and chilli, and cook under a low heat for 3–4 minutes until softened. Add 1 tablespoon of the spice mix and cook for 1 minute.

Step four Add in the potatoes and continue to cook, covered, on a low heat, stirring occasionally, for 20–25 minutes or until the potatoes are cooked through and the outsides have broken up. Season with the lemon, fresh coriander and some salt and pepper, and leave to cool.

Step five Shape the cooled potato mixture around the eggs; you want it to be about 1 cm/½ in thick. Beat the remaining eggs, then coat the potato-covered eggs first in the flour, then the egg and then the breadcrumbs. Heat the oil to 190°C (375°F) for deep-frying. Carefully place the Scotch eggs into the oil and cook for 2–3 minutes or until golden. Scoop out with a slotted spoon and drain on kitchen paper. Serve with a simple cauliflower or carrot purée, seasoned to taste.

Makes 5 eggs

7 eggs

3–4 garlic cloves

3 shallots

3–4cm (1–½ in) piece of fresh root ginger

1 red chilli

1kg (2lb 4oz) Maris Piper potatoes

50g (2oz) butter

1 tbsp rapeseed oil

1 tsp ground turmeric

1 tsp mustard seed

1 tsp ground cumin

juice and zest 1 lemon

a small bunch of fresh coriander

100g (4oz) flour

150g (5oz) soft white breadcrumbs

oil for deep-frying

sea salt and freshly ground black pepper

for the spice mix

1 tbsp coriander seeds

1 tbsp fennel seeds

3 small dried red chillies

1 tsp mustard seeds

1 tsp cumin seeds

1 tsp whole black peppercorns

to serve

cauliflower or carrot purée

Risotto Arancini Balls

A dazzling way to use up any leftover risotto is to make arancini, or stuffed rice balls. Here, I have used the Bright Green Pea and Goats' Cheese Risotto recipe from page159, but this should work with any risotto recipe.

Makes 6 balls

for the filling

175g (6oz) leftover risotto (see page159)

75g (3oz) mozzarella cut into 1cm (½ in) cubes

for the coating

100g (4oz) flour

1 egg, beaten

100 g (4oz) dried white breadcrumbs

sunflower or vegetable oil, for deep-frying

to serve

salad and a wedge of lemon

Step one When the risotto is fridge-cold, scoop out about 25g (1oz) of risotto per ball, and flatten it in the palm of your hand.

Step two Push a cube of mozzarella into the centre of each one and shape the risotto around it like a ball.

Step three In a pan, heat the oil for deep-frying to 180°C (350°F). Dip the balls in the flour, then the egg, and finally the breadcrumbs, and fry for 3–4 minutes until crisp and golden. Serve with salad and a wedge of lemon as a light lunch, starter or snack.

Gnocchi

I recently discovered that the word gnocchi actually means 'dumplings' in Italian, which made me chuckle as there is no better word to describe these little pillows of potato pasta. The great thing about gnocchi is that it's a terrific change from regular pasta and really easy to cook, too.

Step one Boil the unpeeled potatoes in a large pan of water for 25 minutes or until tender. Drain and, when cool enough to handle, remove the skins.

Step two Mash the potatoes until really smooth. Add the egg, the flour and plenty of salt and pepper, and mix to a dough. Turn out and knead on a floured work surface for a few minutes.

Step three Cut the dough into 4 pieces. Roll out each piece into 'ropes' 2cm (¾in) thick (basically long thick strings of dough), then cut each rope into 2.5cm (1in) pieces. Squeeze each piece gently in the middle to make the gnocchi look like little pillows. Leave to dry out for 10 minutes on the floured work surface.

Step four Bring a large pan of salted water to the boil and, working in batches, place the gnocchi into the water. When they rise to the surface, after for 2 minutes or so, lift them out with a slotted spoon. Keep the cooked gnocchi warm while you cook the next batch.

If you are making the gnocchi ahead of time, after shaping them you can leave them out to dry for up to 2 hours. They will also keep in the fridge, uncooked, for 2 days.

Serves 6–8

450g (1lb) medium-sized floury potatoes, not peeled

1 large egg, beaten

250g (9oz) flour ('00' if you can find it, but it's not crucial for gnocchi), plus extra for dusting

sea salt and freshly ground black pepper

For a video masterclass on making fresh pasta, go to
www.mykitchentable.co.uk/videos/makingpasta

Fried Gnocchi with Tomato and Goats' Cheese Sauce

As scrummy as gnocchi are in their own right, frying them gently in butter lifts them to a whole new level. The middles are like fluffy clouds of potato and the outsides become crispy and golden like a potato croquette.

Serves 4

30g (1¼ oz) butter

1 batch freshly made gnocchi (see page 39), or 450g (1lb) fresh shop-bought gnocchi, cooked for 2 minutes in salted, boiling water

freshly grated Parmesan cheese, to serve

for the sauce

1 tbsp olive oil

1 onion, finely chopped

3 garlic cloves, finely chopped

400g (14oz) tin chopped tomatoes

1 tbsp sun-dried tomato paste or tomato purée

a splash of good-quality sherry vinegar

a few splashes of Tabasco

1 tsp sugar

a small bunch fresh basil leaves, torn

100g (4oz) fresh soft goats' cheese

sea salt and freshly ground black pepper

Step one First make the sauce. Heat the oil in a saucepan. Add the onion and fry gently for 8 minutes or until it has softened and begun to turn golden.

Step two Add the garlic and fry for a further minute. Tip in the chopped tomatoes, tomato paste or purée, sherry vinegar, Tabasco, sugar, half the basil and some salt and pepper, and leave to bubble away gently on a low heat for 20 minutes. The sauce will have thickened up nicely by this stage. Crumble in the goats' cheese and stir gently as if to tease it into melting.

Step three Melt the butter in a frying pan and, working in batches, add the precooked gnocchi. Fry for 2 minutes on each side, or until they have crisped up and are golden. Drain the finished gnocchi on kitchen paper while you cook the rest. Serve with a dollop of sauce, the remaining torn basil and a grating of Parmesan.

Stilton Risotto with Sausage, Spring Greens and Crispy Sage

A great, sociable dish to make while nattering to your friends over a glass of wine.

Serves 4

4 Italian pork sausages with fennel

2 tbsp olive oil

1 tbsp butter

1 onion, finely chopped

3 garlic cloves, finely chopped

400g (14oz) risotto rice

1 glass white wine

750ml (1¼ pints) hot chicken or vegetable stock

1 small head of spring greens, outer leaves and stalks removed, then finely sliced

100g (4oz) Stilton

handful of fresh sage leaves

Step one Remove the sausages from their skins. Heat one tablespoon of oil and the butter in a heavy bottomed pan and add the sausages to the pan, breaking them up with a wooden spoon so they resemble small meatballs. It doesn't matter if some of the sausages break up too much; it simply adds to the whole texture. When the sausage is browned remove from the pan with a slotted spoon and drain out any excess oil so there is only about 1 tablespoon left in the pan.

Step two Add the onions and fry over a lowish heat for 10 minutes or until the onions have softened. For the last minute of cooking add the garlic to the pan.

Step three Add the rice and stir for a minute or two to coat the grains of rice. Pour over the glass of wine and keep stirring while the wine is absorbed into the grain. Gradually ladle the hot stock into the risotto letting it absorb between each ladleful. Keep stirring it, too, as this encourages the starch to come out, which is what makes risotto have that creamy texture.

Step four With your last three ladlefuls of stock add in the spring greens. The rice is ready when the grains are cooked but still have a little bite and the rice is loose but not soupy. Add in the Stilton, and watch the risotto become rich and velvety..

Step five In a separate, small frying pan, heat the remaining oil. Add the sage leaves and fry for a minute or two until crisp. Serve the risotto with a scattering of sage leaves.

Aubergine, Artichoke and Lamb Bolognese

To get the best out of this recipe you need to cook the aubergine to the point where it has lost a lot of its water and is quite caramelised, as this will encourage a sweet, sticky sauce.

Serves 4

50ml (2fl oz) olive oil

2 medium aubergines, chopped into 1cm (½ in) cubes

a pinch of salt

550g (1¼ lb) minced lamb

1 onion, finely chopped

4 garlic cloves, finely chopped

300ml (½ pint) white wine

300ml (½ pint) lamb or chicken stock

a small pinch of saffron

400g (14oz) tin chopped tomatoes

2 tbsp tomato purée

a small bunch fresh parsley, stems discarded, leaves chopped

a few fresh thyme sprigs, chopped

4–5 tinned artichokes, drained, then cut into small chunks

350g (12oz) fresh trofie or strozzapreti pasta

to serve

fresh basil leaves

shaved pecorino cheese

Step one Heat the oil in a large, heavy-based pan over a medium-high heat. Sprinkle the aubergines with a little salt, then fry for 15 minutes until softened and browned (it is best to do this in batches). Remove the aubergines with a slotted spoon to leave some oil in the pan. Drain the auergines on kitchen paper.

Step two Add the minced lamb to the pan and season with a little salt. Brown the lamb, then transfer to a bowl with a slotted spoon. Fry the onion in the oil left in the pan for 5–8 minutes or until softened and slightly golden, adding the garlic for the last minute of cooking time.

Step three Return the lamb to the pan and add the white wine, stock, saffron (don't use too much as it can be overpowering), chopped tomatoes, tomato purée, parsley and thyme. Mix well and, when it starts to bubble, add the fried aubergines and the artichokes. Leave to simmer away, partly covered, on a low heat for 1 hour or until the sauce is reduced by one-third.

Step four Ten minutes before you're ready to serve, cook the pasta in lots of boiling, salted water according to the instructions on the packet. (Check it in its last minutes of cooking as it still needs to have some bite.) Drain the pasta and stir through enough sauce to coat. Divide between pasta bowls to serve, and sprinkle with basil and shaved pecorino cheese.

Proper Meat Ragù

Much as everyone loves a good old 'spag bol', going that extra length and making a proper ragù makes all the difference.

Step one Preheat the oven to 170°C/340°F/gas 4. Add the olive oil to a large casserole over a medium heat. Fry the meat in the oil in batches until it is nicely golden brown all over. With a slotted spoon, transfer the meat to a bowl and set aside.

Step two Throw the onions, carrots and celery into the pan and cook on a fairly low heat for 15 minutes, or until the vegetables have softened and gone slightly golden. For the last 2 minutes of cooking add the garlic.

Step three Stir in the tomato purée and cook for a further minute. Add the herbs, wine, stock, tomatoes and half the basil. Return the meat and all its juices to the pan. Stir well, then cover and bake for 2 hours. You want the meat to be really soft and the sauce to thicken and become rich.

Step four Remove the casserole from the oven and leave to rest for 10 minutes, then go to the meat with two forks and shred it to bits. If it is cooked properly, the meat will break up as you squish it a little with the back of a wooden spoon. Meanwhile, bring a large pan of salted water to the boil. Add the pappardelle for and cook it for 2–3 minutes. Drain, then return the pasta to the pan and stir in enough sauce to generously coat it. Serve with the rest of the basil and loads of grated Parmesan.

Serves 4–6

2 tbsp olive oil

400g (14oz) veal or beef shin, chopped into 4cm (1¾ in) cubes

400g (14oz) pork leg, chopped into 4cm (1¾ in) cubes

2 onions, chopped

2 carrots, chopped

2 celery sticks, chopped

4 garlic cloves, chopped

2 tbsp tomato purée

2 bay leaves

a few fresh thyme sprigs, chopped

a fresh rosemary sprig, leaves only, finely chopped

a few fresh parsley sprigs, chopped

400ml (14fl oz) red or white wine

400ml (14fl oz) beef or veal stock

400g (14oz) tin chopped tomatoes

a small bunch fresh basil leaves, torn

300–450g (11oz–1lb) pappardelle, preferably fresh

freshly grated Parmesan cheese, to serve

Creamy Smoked Salmon and Pea Spaghetti

Spaghetti carbonara is a classic for a reason, but it is laden with cream and, therefore, also very guilt-inducing. So I decided to halve the cream content and replace the rest with Greek yoghurt. Having done this, it seemed natural to replace the smokiness of the bacon with smoked salmon. I then decided to add some green colour with the summery addition of broad beans and green peas, my favourite veggies, and finished with a hint of lemon to lift the dish.

Serves 4

350g (12oz) dried spaghetti

150g (5oz) podded and shelled broad beans

150g (5oz) fresh or frozen garden peas

200ml (7fl oz) double cream

200ml (7fl oz) Greek yoghurt

2 large egg yolks

35g (1¼ oz) Parmesan cheese

grated zest of 1 lemon

175g (6oz) smoked salmon (about 8 slices), cut into short ribbons

a small bunch fresh chives, snipped

sea salt and freshly ground black pepper

Step one Bring a large pan of salted water to the boil. Add the spaghetti and cook it according to the instructions on the packet. For the last 3 minutes of the cooking time add the broad beans and peas.

Step two Meanwhile, mix together the cream, yoghurt, egg yolks, Parmesan, lemon zest and some salt and pepper to make a sauce. Drain the cooked pasta, beans and peas, leaving a few tablespoons of water in the bottom of the pan.

Step three Return the pan to a low heat and pour in the sauce. Toss the pasta in the sauce, then add the smoked salmon and chives, mixing well until evenly incorporated and the salmon has cooked through. Serve piping hot.

If you like things quite lemony, add the zest of the whole lemon; otherwise, use just half.

Baked Seafood and Saffron Risotto

This risotto is great for those days when you simply don't have the energy for all that stirring!

Step one Discard any mussels with broken shells or any that do not close when tapped on a hard surface. Scrub them and tug away any hairy beards. To prepare the squid, gently pull the head and tentacles away from the body and clean. Pull out the clear backbone (quill) from inside the body and discard the entrails. Cut the tentacles from the head just below the eyes, then throw the head away. Remove the side wings and the fine membrane from the body. Rinse the body, tentacles and wings thoroughly and pat dry with kitchen paper. Cut the squid body down the centre so it opens out flat, and slice the body and wings into strips 5mm (¼in) wide. Chill the mussels or clams and squid until needed.

Step two Preheat the oven to 180°C/350°F/gas 4. Warm 2 tablespoons of the olive oil in a large casserole over a lowish heat and add the onion and chorizo. Sauté for about 8 minutes, or until the onion has softened and turned slightly golden and the chorizo has released all its oil and coloured slightly. Add the garlic and fry for a further minute.

Step three Stir in the rice and fry for a minute, then pour over the wine and stock. Sprinkle in the saffron and smoked paprika. Cover, place in the oven and bake for 25 minutes.

Step four Remove the casserole from the oven. The rice should by now have absorbed most of the liquid but the mixture will still be a little soupy. Turn the oven up to 200°C/400°F/gas 6. In a bowl, toss the prawns, mussels or clams, squid and monkfish in the remaining tablespoon of olive oil, then give the risotto a good stir and place the seafood on top. Pop the casserole back into the oven, uncovered, and bake for a further 8 minutes. Remove from the oven and sprinkle with parsley. Give it one final stir and it's ready to serve.

Serves 4

8 mussels or clams

1 medium squid

3 tbsp olive oil

1 onion, finely chopped

75g (3oz) semi-dried or fresh chorizo sausage, chopped

3 garlic cloves, chopped

250g (9oz) risotto rice

250ml (8fl oz) white wine

600ml (1 pint) fish, chicken or vegetable stock

a pinch of saffron

a large pinch of smoked paprika

8 raw king prawns, peeled

150g (5oz) monkfish, trimmed and cut into cubes

a small bunch fresh flat-leaf parsley, stems discarded, leaves finely chopped

Slow-cooked Lamb Shoulder Lasagna

Lasagna fan? You might want to try this.

Serves 10

2 tbsp olive oil

800g (1¾lb) lamb shoulder meat, cubed

2 onions, chopped

2 carrots, chopped

2 celery sticks, chopped

1 clove garlic, chopped

2 tbsp tomato purée

2 bay leaves

a few fresh thyme and parsley sprigs, chopped

a fresh rosemary sprig, leaves chopped

fresh basil leaves, torn

400ml (14fl oz) red or white wine

400ml (14fl oz) beef or veal stock

400g (14oz) tin chopped tomatoes

500g (1lb) fresh lasagna sheets

for the white sauce

40g (1½ oz) butter

40g (1½ oz) plain flour

400ml (14fl oz) milk

2 medium-sized balls mozzarella, chopped

freshly grated nutmeg

100g (4oz) Parmesan cheese, grated

sea salt and freshly ground black pepper

Step one Preheat the oven to 160°C/325°F/gas mark 2. Place the oil in a large casserole over a medium heat. Add the meat in batches and fry until it is nicely golden brown all over. Remove with a slotted spoon and set aside. Reduce the heat and throw in the onions, carrots and celery. Cook for 15 minutes or until the vegetables have softened and gone slightly golden. Add the garlic for the last 2 minutes of cooking.

Step two Stir in the tomato purée and cook for 1 minute. Add the herbs, wine, stock and tomatoes. Return the meat and all its juices to the pan. Give it a good stir, then cover and place in the oven. You want the meat to be really soft and the sauce to thicken and become rich. After 2 hours remove the casserole from the oven and leave it to rest for 10 minutes, then go to the meat with two forks and shred it to bits. The meat should break up as you squish it a little with the back of a wooden spoon.

Step three To make the white sauce, melt the butter in a pan over a low to medium heat. Stir in the flour and cook for 1 minute. Take the pan off the heat and gradually whisk in the milk, little by little, stirring like crazy until combined and smooth. Stir in the chopped mozzarella and a few gratings of fresh nutmeg. Season to taste and set aside.

Step four Drop the lasagna sheets into a large pot of boiling water for 1 minute then drain them. Drizzle some olive oil on to the sheets to keep them separate. To build the lasagna, spread a layer of meat sauce over the bottom of a large lasagna dish. Spoon over a little of the white sauce. (The ratio should be about two-thirds meat to one-third white sauce.) Repeat 3 or 4 times, depending on the size of the dish, then spoon over the remaining white sauce to cover completely. Sprinkle with grated Parmesan. Bake for 45–50 minutes until the top is golden.

Butters for Steaks

Butter is one of the best things to have with steak, and it's so easy just mashing a bunch of ingredients together and chilling them before adding a slice to your cooked steak. Here are three of my favourites to try.

Step one Place the butter in a mixing bowl and mash together with the remaining ingredients for your chosen butter. Put between two sheets of clingfilm or greaseproof paper and roll into a tight sausage shape. Chill in the fridge for 2 hours before using and serve along with steak, cooked to your taste.

Garlic and Herb Butter

100g (4oz) unsalted butter, at room temperature

1–2 garlic cloves, grated

50g (2oz) chopped, mixed fresh herbs

sea salt and freshly ground black pepper

Blue Cheese and Toasted Pecan Butter

100g (4oz) unsalted butter, at room temperature

175g (6oz) blue cheese

50g (2oz) toasted pecan nuts, chopped

1 garlic clove, grated

1 tbsp finely chopped fresh chives

sea salt and freshly ground black pepper

Thai Chilli, Lime, Coriander and Mint Butter

100g (4oz) unsalted butter, at room temperature

juice and grated zest of 1 lime

1–2 garlic clove, grated

1 red chilli, seeded and finely chopped

25g (1oz) chopped fresh coriander leaves

25g (1oz) chopped fresh mint leaves

sea salt and freshly ground black pepper

Proper Beef Stew

Sometimes the simplest things are the most delicious. On any cold winter's night a steaming plate of beef stew and mashed potatoes really is good, hearty food at its best.

Serves 4

2 tbsp olive oil

450g (1lb) stewing beef (preferably shin), cut into 4cm (1¾in) chunks

1 onion, chopped

2 carrots, chopped

½ swede, chopped

2 celery sticks, chopped

2 leeks, chopped

1 tsp tomato purée

1 tbsp plain flour

600ml (1 pint) beef stock

2 fresh rosemary sprigs, leaves picked

a few fresh thyme sprigs, leaves picked

2 bay leaves

sea salt and freshly ground black pepper

Step one Preheat the oven to 160°C/325°F/gas 3. To brown the meat, add 1 tablespoon of the oil to a medium-sized, heavy-based casserole over a medium heat. Season the meat, add it to the pan in batches and brown all over. Remove each batch with a slotted spoon and set aside on a plate while you brown the rest.

Step two Reduce the heat under the pan to low and add the remainder of the oil. Stir in the vegetables and cook for 10 minutes or until softened and slightly caramelised.

Step three Stir in the tomato purée and flour and cook for 1 minute. Pour in the stock and return the meat and all its juices to the pan. Stir in the herbs, then cover and bake for 2 hours, or until the meat is falling apart and the sauce has thickened slightly. Season to taste before serving piping hot with mash.

For more recipes from My Kitchen Table, sign up for our newsletter at www.mykitchentable.co.uk/newsletter

KITCHEN TABLE

Japanese Rare Roast Beef Salad with Mixed Radishes

This recipe is based on Japanese beef tataki, a simple seared beef dish. The beef, peppery watercress, radishes, ginger and wasabi dressing all combine to create a flavourful party on your plate.

Step one Heat the oil in a frying pan over a high heat until really hot. Season the steaks with salt and white pepper. Set them in the pan and sear them for 20 seconds on each side. The meat should be fairly dark on the outside and still really rare in the middle. Remove from the pan and leave to rest for 1 hour in the freezer until the meat firms up and is almost frozen.

Step two In a small bowl, mix together the ginger, soy sauce, rice wine vinegar and wasabi paste and set aside.

Step three Remove the beef from the freezer after the hour has gone by and slice thinly. Aim to cut 12 slices from each steak. (You can sneak the end bits as a chef's perk!)

Step four Lay 6 slices of beef, overlapping each other, on each plate. Top with the watercress, tomatoes, a sprinkling of daikon radishes, red radishes and spring onions. Pour over the soy and wasabi sauce. Finally sprinkle with sesame seeds and snipped chives to serve.

Freezing the steaks for an hour after searing them is a restaurant trick that will make the meat easier to slice thinly. Technically you need to let things cool before popping them into the fridge or freezer, but as this meat has only been seared it should not be too warm. Use your own instincts, and if you think it needs to cool a little before freezing, then do so.

Serves 4

1 tbsp olive oil

2 x 200g beef fillet steaks, each 5cm (2in) thick

3cm (1¼ in) piece of fresh root ginger, peeled and grated

2 tbsp soy sauce

2 tbsp rice wine vinegar

1 tsp wasabi paste

1 bunch watercress, trimmed

8 cherry tomatoes, preferably a mixture of red and yellow

5cm (2in) piece white daikon radish, or 8 normal white radishes, peeled and sliced into thin matchsticks

8 red radishes, quartered

2 spring onions, thinly sliced

sea salt and white pepper

to serve

2 tbsp black and white sesame seeds

4 chives, each snipped into 4 pieces

Taleggio and Sage-stuffed Pork Chops with Roasted Apples

You don't get much more British than pork chops, sage and apple! So, I thought I'd throw some Taleggio cheese into the mix. The cheesy melting middle is a scrummy surprise, and the whole thing is drenched in sage butter for some Anglo-Italian magic. Swap the apples for pears and you've got another great dish.

Serves 4

4 Braeburn apples, halved and cored

50g (2oz) butter, plus 8 tsp

handful fresh sage leaves

1 tsp golden caster sugar

4 x 225g pork loin chops, French trimmed (ask your butcher to do this for you)

150g (5oz) Taleggio cheese, cut into 4 long, thin slices

sea salt and freshly ground black pepper

Step one Preheat the oven to 200°C/400°F/gas 6. Place the apple halves on a roasting tin, cut-side up, and place 1 teaspoon of butter on each. Pop a couple of sage leaves on top, and sprinkle with the sugar. Bake for 20 minutes until soft in the middle and crisp and caramelised on the outside.

Step two Meanwhile, slice a pocket into each pork chop along the edge that doesn't have the bone, slicing fairly deeply into the chop, about three-quarters of the way through. Stuff each chop with a slice of Taleggio and a couple more sage leaves. Season with lots of salt and pepper.

Step three Heat half of the remaining butter in a frying pan over a high heat and add the rest of the sage. When it's really hot (but not so hot that it begins to burn), add the chops and fry for 2 minutes. Turn the chops over, add the last of the butter and cook for a further 2 minutes. Transfer the chops to the same roasting tin as the apples. Pour over the sage butter and roast for a further 5 minutes.

Step four Remove the tin from the oven and leave to rest for 5 minutes. By now the chops will be oozing with melting cheese. Serve each chop with 2 apple halves and some of the buttery juices poured over.

Parma Ham and Sage-wrapped Veal with Tomato Spaghetti

My sisters and I were brought up on veal Milanese, and I wanted to bring the dish into the twenty-first century.

Step one Put the sage leaves and bread into a food-processor and whizz until you have fragrant breadcrumbs.

Step two Lay the veal escalopes on a chopping board. Cover each with a couple sheets of clingfilm. Using a meat tenderiser or a rolling pin, bash each one until it is about 2–3mm (just under ¼in) thick. Uncover and wrap each escalope in Parma ham (you may need to use some of the beaten egg to stick these down). Season the flour with salt and pepper, then put the flour, egg and breadcrumbs into separate shallow bowls. Dip each escalope into the flour, then coat with the beaten egg and finally with breadcrumbs. Chill the escalopes while you prepare the rest of the dish.

Step three To make the spaghetti sauce, heat the tablespoon of oil in a large pan over a low heat. Throw in the onion and cook for 8 minutes, or until softened. For the last minute of cooking, add the garlic. Then add the tinned tomatoes, tomato purée, sugar, vinegar and basil. Season with salt and pepper and leave to bubble away for 20 minutes. Halfway through, get the spaghetti cooking in plenty of boiling salted water.

Step four Once the spaghetti is on, heat the 100ml (4fl oz) of oil in a frying pan over a medium heat. Carefully lay the breaded escalopes into the oil (if they are very large you may need to cook them one at a time). Fry the escalopes for 3 minutes on each side or until the breadcrumb coating is golden brown then drain on kitchen paper. Drain the spaghetti and mix with the tomato sauce. Serve the spaghetti with the veal, some lemon wedges and a shaving of Parmesan cheese if you like.

Serves 4

20 fresh sage leaves

100g (4oz) fresh white bread, crusts removed

4 x 150g (5oz) veal escalopes, preferably British rose veal

4 slices Parma ham

1 large egg, lightly beaten

100g (4oz) plain flour

100ml (4fl oz) olive oil

sea salt and freshly ground black pepper

for the spaghetti

1 tbsp olive oil

1 small onion, finely chopped

3 garlic cloves, finely chopped

2 x 400g (14oz) tins cherry tomatoes

1 tbsp tomato purée

1 tsp golden caster sugar

a splash of sherry vinegar

a small bunch fresh basil, finely chopped

350g (12oz) spaghetti

to serve

lemon wedges

Parmesan cheese

Milk-roasted Pork with Cinnamon, Orange and Bay

It sounds surprising, but milk tenderises pork. Be careful not to overcook it though. Ask your butcher to 'French trim' the pork for you. It looks beautiful.

Serves 6

1kg (2¼ lb) pork loin

1 tbsp ground coriander

1 tbsp fennel seeds

2 tbsp olive oil

570ml (1 pint) full-fat milk, or 1 tbsp double cream mixed into 550ml (18fl oz) semi-skimmed milk

1 cinnamon stick

grated zest of 1 orange

3 bay leaves

1 tsp plain flour

400ml (14fl oz) chicken stock

1 tbsp double cream (optional)

sea salt and freshly ground black pepper

Step one Preheat the oven to 180°C/350°F/gas 4. If your butcher has not already done it, slash the crackling fat with a sharp knife. Mix together the coriander, fennel seeds and some salt and pepper and rub this all over the meat. Heat the oil over a medium heat in the smallest roasting tin the pork will fit into. Lay the meat fat-side down and fry the fat first – it may spit, so be careful. Brown the pork all over, then remove it from the heat.

Step two Pour the milk into the roasting tin and add the cinnamon, orange zest and bay leaves. Roast for 1½ hours, basting the pork with the milk every 25 minutes. The milk will reduce during the cooking. When it is time to remove the pork from the oven, you should be able to poke a skewer into it and, when you take it out, the juices should run clear. The crackling should be lovely and crisp, but if it isn't quite there yet, slice it off the meat, place it on a roasting tin and put it back into the oven for 10 minutes. Leave the pork to rest for 20 minutes. Then remove it from the tin and leave to rest for a further 10 minutes on a plate.

Step three Pour the milky porky residue and aromatics remaining in the tin into a small pan on a low heat. Whisk in the flour and heat until it begins to bubble. Stir in the stock little by little, then leave it to simmer away for 2–3 minutes, or until the sauce has begun to thicken.

Step four Sieve the sauce to get the aromatics and any larger lumps out. It will still have fine lumps and if this really bothers you, stir in a tablespoon of double cream. Season the sauce. You should get hits of all the flavours, with natural added sweetness from the milk. Serve the pork cut between the bones like chops, with a drizzle of sauce.

Basic Roasted Five-spice Pork Belly

This is a great dish to have in your repertoire! Anyone who has eaten pork belly knows that there is not much out there that matches its glorious meltness. Perfect pork belly always has crisp crackling and meat so tender it falls apart under your fork. Most pork belly recipes call for the pork to be rubbed with crushed cumin seeds and roasted, but pork belly is also a popular Asian ingredient and adores spices. So here I have rubbed the pork belly with Chinese five-spice powder, a mixture of cinnamon, star anise, Sichuan pepper, cloves and the pork classic, fennel seeds. Then I slowly roast the pork until it falls apart.

Step one Preheat the oven to 230°C/450°F/gas 8. Rub the pork all over with olive oil and then rub on the five-spice powder and some salt and pepper. Place the pork on a rack in a roasting tin and roast for 20 minutes.

Step two Reduce the oven temperature to 180°C/350°F/gas 4 and roast for a further 1½ hours. Remove from the oven and leave to rest for 15 minutes before carving. If the crackling isn't crisp enough, slice it off in one piece and return it to the oven on a high heat for 15 minutes while you rest the pork under foil.

Serves 8

1.5kg (3lb) belly pork, with an even thickness, and rind scored (ask your butcher to do this)

1 tbsp olive oil

1 tbsp Chinese five-spice powder

sea salt and freshly ground black pepper

Have you made this recipe? Tell us what you think at
www.mykitchentable.co.uk/blog

Roasted Pork Belly with Apple, Plum and Star Anise Sauce

We all know that pork and apple sauce is a winner, but with pork belly infused with Chinese five-spice, I wanted to see if I could come up with an Asian-style apple sauce. With the addition of plums, star anise and soy, I do believe I've nailed it.

Serves 4

1 x Basic Roasted Five-spice Pork Belly (see page 67)

2 Bramley apples, peeled and chopped

2 red plums, stoned and chopped

1 tbsp soy sauce

1 star anise

1 tbsp golden caster sugar

1 tbsp plain flour

1 glass white wine

200ml (7fl oz) chicken stock

300g (10¼ oz) tenderstem broccoli

Step one Prepare the roasted pork belly. While it is roasting, place the apples, plums, soy sauce, star anise and caster sugar in a pan over a low heat and cook gently for about 15 minutes. Remove from the heat and leave to cool.

Step two After the meat has roasted and is resting on a plate, make a light gravy. Tip the excess fat, bar about a tablespoon, out of the roasting tin. Place the tin over a low heat and stir the flour, scraping away at the residue on the bottom. Let the flour cook for a minute then slowly pour in the wine while continuing to scrape the pan. Once all the wine is added you may want to switch to a whisk in order to avoid getting lumps in your gravy. Whisk in the stock, bring to the boil and cook for about 5 minutes, or until slightly thickened. Strain into a gravy boat.

Step three Steam or boil the broccoli for 3 minutes. To serve, slice the pork and serve it with the broccoli, some gravy poured over and a big dollop of the Asian apple, plum and star anise sauce on the side. This goes really well with creamy mashed potato. (See page 144.)

Spiced Mango-roasted Ham

Most butchers nowadays will tell you it's unnecessary to soak a ham, so don't be put off making this if you don't have enough time to soak the ham overnight.

Step one Put the ham into the biggest pot you can find, preferably a deep, wide stockpot into which it will fit easily. Place it over a medium heat and pour in the mango juice. Add the onions, carrots, leeks, spices and bay leaves and top up with water to cover. Slowly bring the liquid to the boil. Using a large spoon, carefully remove any scum that appears and repeat until the surface looks clear.

Step two Once the liquid is bubbling, reduce the heat to a fast simmer for 3 hours. Top up regularly with cold water and remove any scum from the surface every time you do so.

Step three Preheat the oven to 180°C/350°F/gas 4. Once the ham is cooked (it will start to pull away from the bone), remove it from the pan very carefully so as not to tear any of the meat. (You may find it easier to let the ham cool a little in the cooking liquor, then transfer it to a colander to allow it to drain and cool for 10 minutes.) Place the ham in a large roasting tin. Very carefully, slice the skin to reveal the thick layer of white fat, then score the fat crossways in both directions so there are loads of little diamond shapes all over it.

Step four Add all the glaze ingredients, except for the cloves, to a pan over a medium heat. Stir until everything has melted. Allow to cool slightly then rub all over the ham. Push a clove into the corners of each diamond shape. This not only makes the ham look really beautiful, but the cloves release the most amazing aroma as the ham cooks. Roast for 40 minutes, until sticky and caramelised. Leave it to rest for 1 hour if you want to eat it warm, or let it cool completely. Serve with mashed or boiled new potatoes, salad and chutneys and pickles.

Serves 10–15

1.5kg (3lb) smoked, boned and rolled gammon ham, soaked overnight in loads of cold water (change the water a few times)

1 litre (1¾ pints) mango juice

2 medium onions, quartered

2 carrots, halved

2 leeks (whites only), halved lengthways

6 whole cloves

2 star anise

8 allspice berries

10 black peppercorns

2 bay leaves

for the glaze

4 tbsp mango chutney

2 tbsp butter

1 tsp mixed spice

1 tsp smoked paprika

50 whole cloves

to serve

new potatoes, mashed or boiled

salad

chutneys and pickles

Lamb Massaman Curry

Wow your dinner party guests with your knowledge of Asian ingredients.

Serves 4

450g (1lb) lamb neck fillet

2 x 400g (14oz) tins coconut milk

400ml (14fl oz) lamb or chicken stock

2 tbsp brown sugar

8 smallish new potatoes

sea salt and freshly ground black pepper

for the curry paste

2.5cm (1in) piece fresh root ginger

2 stalks lemongrass,

4 shallots, sliced

5 garlic cloves, peeled

2 red chillies, chopped

1 tbsp ground coriander

1 tsp ground cumin

½ tsp grated nutmeg

½ tsp ground cinnamon

¼ tsp ground cloves

4 cardamom pods, crushed

2 tbsp Thai fish sauce

1 tsp shrimp paste

3 tbsp groundnut oil

to serve

3 tbsp toasted crushed peanuts

fresh coriander

hot cooked rice

Step one Make the paste by peeling and slicing the ginger. Remove and discard the tough outer leaves from the lemongrass and chop roughly. Add the ginger, lemongrass and the remaining paste ingredients to a blender and blitz for 30 seconds until smooth. Heat a wok or large frying pan (one with a lid) over a medium heat, pour in the paste and stir-fry for 1 minute to awaken the flavours.

Step two Cut the lamb into 2.5cm (1in) cubes. Raise the heat under the wok to high and add the meat. Stir-fry for a good 5 minutes, until the meat is coated in the paste. You want to try to get some colour on the meat, so make sure the heat is quite high, but not so high that the paste burns. Add the coconut milk, stock and brown sugar, then reduce the heat, cover and leave to bubble away very gently for 45 minutes.

Step three Add the potatoes, cover, and continue cooking gently for a further 45 minutes. The curry is ready when the lamb is meltingly tender and the potatoes are cooked through. Season to taste. Scatter peanuts and fresh coriander on top of the curry and serve with rice.

Lamb Chops with Green Peppercorn Sauce

But green peppercorn sauce is for beef, I hear you say! Traditionally yes, but one day I was craving peppercorn sauce and only had lamb chops at home, which is how I discovered that it is great with lamb as well. Somehow this usually rich and indulgent sauce becomes lighter and more fragrant. Give it a go – I know you'll be swayed. As you'd expect, this sauce is also excellent with steak.

Step one Rub the chops with the olive oil and season with salt and pepper. Heat a large griddle pan over a high heat and, when the pan is hot, add the chops and cook for 2 minutes on each side for medium rare (or until cooked to your liking). Set the chops aside to keep warm while you make the sauce.

Step two Put the brandy and peppercorns into a sauté pan over a medium-high heat and bring to the boil. Reduce the heat slightly and let the brandy bubble away for 3 minutes, or until syrupy. Add the stock and continue to simmer for about 10 minutes, until reduced by half. Stir in the cream and boil for a further 3 minutes, then whisk in the butter and parsley. When the sauce is becoming thick and glossy, place a couple of chops on each plate. Spoon over the sauce and serve immediately with a green salad.

Serves 4

8 x 150g (5oz) lamb chops

1 tsp olive oil

sea salt and freshly ground black pepper

for the sauce

240ml (8fl oz) brandy

3 tbsp green peppercorns in brine, drained, half of them chopped

480ml (16fl oz) lamb or beef stock

240ml (8fl oz) double cream

large knob cold butter

a small bunch fresh parsley, chopped

green salad, to serve

Breaded Lamb Cutlets with Salsa Verde

The salsa verde is to die for, with a herby, citrusy tang, the anchovies just adding enough seasoning to carry the dish and give it backbone.

Serves 4

2 racks of lamb

100g (4oz) plain flour

1 egg, lightly beaten

200g (7oz) fresh breadcrumbs

a small handful fresh mint leaves, finely chopped

1 tbsp capers, finely chopped

100ml (4fl oz) olive oil

sea salt and freshly ground black pepper

for the salsa verde

1–2 garlic cloves, peeled

a small handful capers

a small handful pickled gherkins

6 anchovy fillets

2 large handfuls fresh flat-leaf parsley

a handful fresh basil leaves

a handful fresh mint leaves

1 tbsp Dijon mustard

3 tbsp sherry vinegar

juice of ½ lemon

150ml (¼ pint) best-quality olive oil

sea salt and freshly ground black pepper

Step one Cut the rack of lamb into cutlets and lay them on a board. Place a double sheet of clingfilm over the top of each one and bash them with a meat tenderiser or rolling pin to flatten them to about 5mm (¼in) thick.

Step two Season the flour with lots of salt and pepper. Set out the flour, egg and breadcrumbs in separate shallow bowls. Add the chopped mint and capers to the breadcrumbs and mix thoroughly. Dip each cutlet first into the flour, then into the egg, and finally into the breadcrumbs. Set the breaded cutlets aside for a few minutes while you make the salsa verde.

Step three Place all the salsa verde ingredients into a food-processor and blitz. Pour the 100ml (4fl oz) oil into a frying pan over a medium-high heat. Add the breaded cutlets, in batches if necessary, and cook for 2 minutes on each side, or until the crumbs have turned golden brown. You want the cutlets to be pink inside, so be careful not to overcook them. Transfer the cooked cutlets to some kitchen paper to drain while you fry the rest. Allow 3–4 cutlets per person and serve with a little dish of salsa verde on the side of each plate.

When it comes to selecting the lamb, either go for the middle neck, which is cheaper and has more flavour, but only 5 bones, or best end of neck, which is more delicate and more expensive, but has 8 bones.

Greek Lamb Shanks with Tomatoes and Orzo

The Greeks do lamb brilliantly, and this one-pot casserole is exemplary of this and packed with classic Greek ingredients. Some dishes are worth a bit of patience, and this one is worth that extra bit of time it takes to cook and develop super flavours and an aroma that will drive you wild.

Serves 4

4 lamb shanks

3 tsp olive oil

2 onions, thinly sliced

1 whole bulb of garlic, cut in half widthways

¼ tsp dried oregano, or 1 tsp chopped fresh oregano

8 vine-ripened tomatoes, chopped

300ml (½ pint) dry white wine

600ml fresh chicken stock

300g (11oz) orzo pasta

zest and juice of ½ lemon

a small bunch fresh flat-leaf parsley, finely chopped

sea salt and freshly ground black pepper

freshly grated Parmesan cheese, to serve

Step one Preheat oven to 200°C/400°F/gas 6. Rub the shanks generously with salt and pepper. Add the oil to a large casserole over a medium heat and brown the shanks on all sides in the oil for about 5 minutes. Transfer the shanks to a plate, then stir the onions and garlic into the pan. Cook for 10 minutes until the onions have softened but not really achieved much colour.

Step two Sprinkle over the oregano, add the tomatoes and wine and bring to the boil. Reduce this mixture for 10 minutes or until the tomatoes have broken up and have dried out a little. Return the shanks to the pan and cover with the stock. Cover the casserole and pop it into the oven for 30 minutes, then reduce the temperature to 170°C/338°F/gas 3 and continue to roast for 1½ hours.

Step three Remove the casserole from the oven, uncover, and add the orzo. Give it a stir, cover and return to the oven for a further 30 minutes, or until the orzo has swollen up and become al dente. Remove from the oven, transfer the shanks to 4 serving plates and keep warm. Add the lemon zest and juice, the chopped parsley and some salt and pepper to the casserole and stir it in. Divide the mixture among the 4 serving plates, scatter with Parmesan and serve.

Chilli Con Carne with Avocado, Soured Cream and Coriander

Chilli is the ultimate dish to whip up when you have your mates over.

Serves 6

1 large onion

3–5 garlic cloves

1 fresh red chilli

2 tbsp olive oil

450g (1lb) minced beef

400g (14 oz) tin chopped tomatoes

2 tbsp tomato purée

2 bay leaves

1 tsp dried oregano

½ heaped tsp cayenne pepper

2 tbsp ground cumin

1 tbsp ground coriander

1 tsp mild chilli powder

600ml (1 pint) beef stock

sea salt

450g (1lb) Basmati rice

400g (14oz) tin red kidney beans, drained and rinsed

to serve

1 ripe avocado

300ml (½ pint) soured cream

150g (5oz) Cheddar

jalapeno peppers

a small bunch fresh coriander, chopped

Step one Finely chop the onion and the garlic cloves and seed and chop the chilli. Place the oil in a large pan on a medium heat. Add the minced beef and brown it. Remove the mince with a slotted spoon, leaving as much fat in the pan as possible. Add the chopped onions and cook gently for 8 minutes or until the onions have softened and started to turn golden. For the last minute, add the garlic and chilli.

Step two Add the chopped tomatoes, tomato purée, bay leaves, oregano, cayenne pepper, cumin, ground coriander, chilli powder, stock and some salt. Mix well, cover the pan and simmer for 1 hour. Towards the end of the hour, cook the Basmati rice according to the instructions on the packet.

Step three After the chilli has cooked for an hour add the kidney beans. Cook, covered, for 15 minutes, or until the chilli is rich and reduced. Meanwhile, peel, stone and chop the avocado, and grate the Cheddar cheese and place them in serving dishes. Whack the chilli on the table in the casserole dish along with the rice and all the other accompaniments and tuck in!

Venison Sausage, Panchetta and Lentil Casserole

Venison can scare people if they are not used to eating game, but a great way of giving it a go is to have a venison sausage. In this dish, the lentils suck up all of the flavours in the pan and the sausages stay fat and juicy. This would be a cracking dish to serve up at a dinner party, and it's one of the best one-pot, great-value dishes I can think of.

Step one Heat the oil in a large casserole. Add the sausages and brown them all over. Remove from the pan then add the pancetta. Fry for a minute or two, then add the shallots, carrots and garlic cloves. Fry for about 5 minutes or until the pancetta is golden and becoming crisp and the carrots, shallots and garlic have some colour. For the last minute of cooking add the chilli flakes and herbs.

Step two Add the tomato purée and cook for a further minute. Stir in the lentils, then cover with the port and stock. Bring to the boil, then reduce the heat to a simmer. Return the sausages to the pan, cover and leave to simmer for 30 minutes or until the lentils have absorbed most of the stock. Stir in the redcurrant jelly and serve sprinkled with the chopped parsley.

Serves 4

1 tbsp olive oil

8 venison sausages

150g (5oz) cubed pancetta

8 medium shallots, cut in half

2 carrots, cut into chunks

8 garlic cloves, peeled but left whole

a pinch of dried chilli flakes

a fresh rosemary sprig

a few fresh thyme sprigs

1 tsp tomato purée

250g (9oz) Puy or green lentils

300ml (½ pint) port

600ml (1 pint) fresh chicken stock

1 tsp redcurrant jelly

½ a small bunch of fresh parsley, roughly chopped

The Ultimate Steak and Stilton Sandwich

A good steak sandwich is not to be missed, but with the inclusion of Stilton its deliciousness becomes stratospheric! It's worth spending the time to make the caramelised onions, but no one is going to frown at you if you cheat with some onion marmalade instead.

Serves 4

for the caramelised onions

2 tbsp olive oil, plus extra for drizzling

1 large red onion, finely sliced

for the steak sandwiches

2 sirloins or rump steaks, about 200g (7oz) each

4 mini ciabatta or crusty rolls

100g (4oz) Stilton cheese

100g (4oz) watercress

2 tsp English mustard

sea salt and freshly ground black pepper

Step one Heat the olive oil in a frying pan, add the onion and season. Cook on a medium heat for 10–15 minutes until golden and caramelized. Remove from the heat and set aside.

Step two Heat a griddle pan until smoking. Season the steaks well with salt and pepper then griddle (chargrill) for 2–3 minutes each side for rare or medium. Transfer the steaks to a plate and leave to rest for 10 minutes.

Step three Slice the rolls in half horizontally. Place them on the griddle cut-face down for a minute until a little charred. Whip them off the grill, then drizzle with a little olive oil. Cut the steaks into slices about 1cm (½in) thick. To serve, fill each roll with steak slices, Stilton, watercress, caramelised onions and some mustard.

my

KITCHEN TABLE

For a video masterclass on how to chop an onion, go to www.mykitchentable.co.uk/videos/choppingonion

Sausage, Sage and Apple 'Wellington'

Beef Wellington meets a sausage roll. What's not to love?

Step one In a bowl mix together the sausage meat, sage, onion, apple, the whole egg and some salt and pepper. Place the mixture on a plate and shape it into a giant sausage 20cm (8in) long and 7.5cm (3in) thick. Cover with cling film and chill.

Step two Heat the oil in a pan, add the shallots and sauté for 2 minutes. Add the mushrooms and fry for 10 minutes or until softened. In the last minute of cooking, add the garlic and thyme leaves. Remove from the heat and leave to cool for 10 minutes.

Step three Lay out a 40cm (16in) long double layer of clingfilm, then place another double layer of cling film next to it, overlapping the other sheets by about 10cm (4in) so you have a large surface area of clingfilm. Lay six slices of the Parma ham along the centre, overlapping each slice with the next. Lay the next six slices in the same way above this layer to elongate the layer of ham. Spread the mushrooms all over the ham. Place the sausage at the base of the ham and mushrooms then, with the help of the clingfilm, roll the ham all around the sausage as tightly as you can. Tie the ends of the clingfilm and chill for 30 minutes.

Step four Dust your work surface with flour and roll out the pastry into a rectangle measuring 40 x 30cm (16 x 12in). Unravel the ham-wrapped sausage from its clingfilm, making sure you do not unwrap the ham. With the widest side of pastry towards you, lay the sausage at the bottom end of the pastry. Roll the pastry over the ham-wrapped sausage. Trim off any excess on the sides and tuck the pastry under. Reroll the excess pastry and cut out some shapes for decorations. Brush the beaten egg yolk over the pastry. Place the shapes on top of the pastry, and then glaze these too. Chill for 30 minutes. Meanwhile, preheat the oven to 200°C/400°F/gas 6. Remove the Wellington from the fridge and bake for 35 minutes or until the pastry is golden and crisp. Leave to rest for 15 minutes before cutting into slices and serving.

Serves 4

400g (14oz) sausage meat

5 fresh sage sprigs, stems discarded, leaves chopped

1 onion, peeled and grated

2 apples, peeled and grated

1 egg, plus 2 egg yolks

2 tbsp olive oil

2 banana shallots, finely chopped

5 field or portobello mushrooms, finely chopped

3 garlic cloves, finely chopped

leaves from a few fresh thyme sprigs

12 slices of Parma ham

flour, for dusting

1 x 500g packet all-butter puff pastry

sea salt and freshly ground black pepper

Beef Wellington

In our house, beef Wellington is the number-one requested dish.

Serves 8

1kg (2¼ lb) (or a 25cm/10in-long piece) beef fillet, taken from the middle to thick end

2 tbsp olive oil

2 banana shallots, finely chopped

5 field or portobello mushrooms, finely chopped

3 garlic cloves, finely chopped

leaves from a few fresh thyme sprigs

1 tsp truffle oil (optional)

½ small bunch flat-leaf parsley, chopped

12 slices Parma ham

flour, for dusting

1 x 500g packet all-butter puff pastry

2 large egg yolks, beaten

sea salt and freshly ground black pepper

Step one Generously season the beef fillet with salt and black pepper. Heat 1 tablespoon of the oil in a frying pan and brown the meat all over for about 8 minutes. Set aside to cool.

Step two Heat the remaining oil in the same pan, add the shallots and sauté for 2 minutes. Add the mushrooms and fry for 10 minutes, or until they have softened and gone brown. For the last minute of cooking, add the garlic, thyme, truffle oil (if using) and parsley. Remove from the heat and leave to cool for 10 minutes.

Step three Lay out a double layer of clingfilm 40cm (16in) long. Then lay another double layer of clingfilm beside it, overlapping the first by 10cm (4in) so you have a large rectangular grid of film. Starting at the bottom of the long side, lay six slices of Parma ham centrally, overlapping each slice with the next. Lay the next six slices in the same way above this layer to double the width.

Step four Spread the mushrooms over the ham. Place the beef at one end of the ham and mushrooms then roll the beef in the ham. Wrap the clingfilm round the beef and roll it tight, tying the ends like a cracker. Chill in the fridge for 30 minutes.

Step five Dust a work surface with flour, then roll out the pastry into a rectangle measuring 40 x 30cm (16 x 12in). Unravel the ham-wrapped beef carefully from its clingfilm. With the widest side of the pastry towards you, lay the beef at the bottom edge of the pastry. Roll the beef in the pastry. Trim off any excess from the sides and tuck the pastry under the beef. Cut excess pastry into shapes such as leaves or stars. and place on top. Using a pastry brush, brush the beaten egg yolk over the pastry. Chill in the fridge for 30 minutes. Meanwhile, preheat the oven to 200°C/400°F/gas 6.

Step six Remove the Wellington from the fridge and bake for 35 minutes, or until the pastry is golden and crisp. Leave to rest for 15 minutes before serving.

Super-duper Sausage Rolls

We all love a good sausage roll, but eating one made from scratch is a whole different experience. These are truly spectacular, and what's really nice is that you can fill each roll with your favourite chutney or even ketchup for the kids before baking, so you get a lovely, oozy sauce with each bite. I think they are just wonderful eaten hot, but they're equally delicious eaten cold the next day. You could even try serving them hot as a main course, with mashed potato and onion gravy.

Step one Place the sausage meat into a large bowl and add the grated onion, chopped sage leaves, Parmesan (if using), a light grating of nutmeg and some salt and pepper, and set aside.

Step two Dust a work surface with flour and roll out the pastry into an oblong shape the thickness of a 50p coin. Cut the pastry into three wide strips and spread 1 tablespoon chutney or ketchup along each strip.

Step three Divide the sausage meat mixture into three and form into three long sausages the same length as the pastry strips. Place them on the pastry, brush the pastry edges with the beaten egg, fold the pastry over the sausagemeat and seal the edges. Turn the roll over onto the folded side and brush all over with the egg. Make lots of little slashes on the surface of the rolls with a small knife, then chill in the fridge for 30 minutes. Meanwhile, preheat the oven to 200°C/400°F/gas 6.

Step four Place the sausage rolls on a board and cut them into individual rolls, cutting each long roll either into thirds or into lots of small, bite-sized rolls. Set them on a baking sheet and bake for 20 minutes for the small ones, 30 minutes for the larger ones. Remove from the oven and leave to cool for 10 minutes.

Makes 9 medium-sized sausage rolls or lots of smaller ones

450g (1lb) good-quality pork sausage meat or 450g (1lb) pork sausages, meat squeezed out of the casing

1 medium onion, peeled and grated

2 fresh sage sprigs, stems discarded, leaves chopped

1 tbsp grated Parmesan cheese (optional)

fresh grated nutmeg

flour, for dusting

1 x 500g packet all-butter pastry

3 tbsp chutney or ketchup

1 large egg, lightly beaten

sea salt and freshly ground black pepper

Chicken Meatball Chasseur with Tagliatelle

Chicken chasseur was one of the first things I ever learnt how to cook, then when I hit catering school it was one of the first things we learnt there too. I think it is a staple recipe that everyone should have under their belt. In this variation I have used meatballs and served them with buttered tagliatelle, which is not only super delicious but also reduces the cooking time so you can have it from fridge to table in 35 minutes, making it even more accessible for everyday cooking. Try it with turkey too, it's a keeper!

Serves 4

½ tsp of mixed sea salt and freshly ground black pepper

500g (18oz) free-range chicken mince

30g plain flour

2 tbsp olive oil

12 small shallots, peeled

2 garlic cloves, peeled and finely chopped

175g chestnut mushrooms, cut into quarters

a few thyme sprigs

100ml (3½ fl oz) Madeira

300ml (½ pint) fresh chicken stock

100ml (3½ fl oz) Passata

100ml (3½ fl oz) double cream

a few fresh tarragon sprigs, torn

400g (14 oz) fresh egg tagliatelle, to serve, dressed in butter and poppy seeds

Step one Season the minced chicken with the salt and pepper and with your hands give a really good mix breaking up the mince as you go to get all the seasoning covering the meat. Shape into small meatballs, about the size of a ping-pong ball. Coat the balls in the flour.

Step two Heat a large casserole pot and add half the olive oil. Once hot, put in the floured chicken meatballs. Cook over a medium to high heat for 4–5 minutes, until golden brown turning occasionally. Remove and leave to rest. You may need to do this in batches.

Step three Put the rest of the olive oil in the casserole pot and add the shallots. Cook for 3 minutes until they begin to soften and go golden. Add the garlic and cook for 2 minutes, then add the mushrooms and thyme. Cook for a further 2 minutes. Pour in the Madeira and rub the bottom of the pan to scrape up all the flavour. Return the meatballs and add the chicken stock and passata. Bring to the boil, then reduce to a simmer and cook for 20 minutes.

Step four Just before serving, add the cream to the chicken chasseur in the casserole pot and simmer for a further 5 minutes to reduce. Place a mound of pasta on to each plate and serve the chicken meatballs chasseur alongside. Spoon over the delicious sauce and garnish with the fresh tarragon.

My Mum's Chorizo, Pepper and Rice Stuffing for Chicken

Easter-time in our household was always heralded by my mum's rice-stuffed roast chicken. She used smoked bacon but I prefer to use chorizo, because I like the stuffing to be spicy, and the orange hue of the chorizo makes the dish so vibrant. While the chicken cooks and rests, the chorizo oozes its juices into the rice, making it doubly delicious. The fab thing about this stuffing is that it doubles up as a side dish, so you can either serve it as a stuffing or have a spoonful of the fragrant rice with some crisp green salad. For instructions on roasting a chicken, see page 111.

Step one Heat the oil in a frying pan over a lowish heat. Add the chorizo and sauté for 1–2 minutes. Add the onions and cook gently for 8 minutes, or until they have softened and the chorizo is starting to char. The onions will be bright orange because of all of the paprika juices from the chorizo. Add the garlic in the last minute of cooking.

Step two Add the red peppers, thyme leaves and smoked paprika and continue sauté for 1 minute. Add the cooked rice and parsley and toss everything together. Leave to cool for 30 minutes and the stuffing is ready.

1 tbsp olive oil

2 fresh chorizo sausages, chopped

1 onion, finely chopped

3 garlic cloves, finely chopped

2 roasted red peppers, from a jar or the deli counter, chopped

leaves from a few fresh thyme sprigs

½ tsp smoked paprika

200g (7oz) cooked white, brown or wild rice

a small bunch fresh flat-leaf parsley, chopped

sea salt and freshly ground black pepper

Chicken Marinades

Marinades are marvellous. All they need is a little thought and you can turn a bog standard piece of chicken into a piece of scrumptiousness.

Fiery Jerk Marinade

2 tbsp English mustard

2 tbsp red wine vinegar

zest and juice of 2 limes

4 tbsp clear honey

3 habanero (Scotch bonnet) chillies, seeded and chopped

6 spring onions, roughly chopped

5 garlic cloves, chopped

a few fresh sprigs of thyme

a few fresh sprigs of oregano

½ tsp sea salt

Peri Peri Marinade

juice of 2 limes

juice of 2 lemons

1 tsp paprika

1 tsp angostura bitters (optional)

1 tsp Tabasco sauce

1 chipotle chilli, soaked for 2 hours in boiling water, then stalk removed

2 garlic cloves, chopped

1 red chilli, seeded and chopped

2 tbsp clear honey

Step one Place all the ingredients in a food processor and blitz until smooth. Coat the chicken and leave to marinate for at least 2 hours, but preferably overnight.

For a video masterclass on marinating meat, go to www.mykitchentable.co.uk/videos/marinatingmeat

(Slightly Better for You) Southern Fried Chicken (and Gravy)

I have a weakness for takeaway Southern fried chicken. Recreating it yourself at home with a healthier approach makes this kinda good for you. Well, at least that's what I'm going to tell myself. The American-style chicken gravy you make in this recipe is much thicker than ours, somewhere between a gravy and white sauce, I'd say.

Step one Mix the buttermilk or yoghurt with the milk in a bowl. Add the chicken and stir to coat. Some people believe you should marinate the chicken in this mixture for 20–30 minutes to tenderise it. In another bowl mix together the flour, seasoning and spices.

Step two Heat the oil in a deep frying pan or sauté pan until it's shimmering. Toss the chicken in the spiced flour, making sure it gets a really good thick coating. Add the chicken pieces to the oil in batches and fry for 4–5 minutes on each side, or until crisp, golden and cooked through. Remove the chicken with a slotted spoon and drain on kitchen paper while you cook the rest of the chicken. Don't throw away the leftover seasoned flour.

Step three To make the gravy, pour the oil into a heatproof container, leaving about 1 tablespoon plus all the crispy bits in the bottom of the pan. Stir in 1 tablespoon of the leftover spiced flour and cook, stirring, for 1 minute. Gradually stir in the chicken stock, stirring until the gravy is smooth. Bring to the boil, then simmer until thicken and reduced. There is quite a lot of seasoning in the flour, so you will not need any salt.

To make purple coleslaw to serve with the chicken, finely slice ½ red onion and mix well in a bowl with 100g (4oz) thinly sliced red cabbage, 100g (4oz) thinly sliced white cabbage, ½ bulb of fennel, thinly sliced, 6 thinly sliced radishes, 100ml (4fl oz) Greek yoghurt, 1½ tbsp red wine vinegar, ½ tsp celery seeds, ½ tsp fennel seeds, salt and pepper.

Serves 4

300ml (½ pint) buttermilk or natural yoghurt

a splash of milk

3–4 skinless, boneless chicken breasts, each cut into 6 or 7 pieces

100g (4oz) plain flour

¾ tsp sea salt

½ tsp ground white pepper

½ tsp freshly ground black pepper

½ tsp celery salt

½ tsp cayenne pepper

½ tsp paprika (use hot paprika if you want it spicy)

150–200ml (5–6½ fl oz) olive oil

400ml (14fl oz) chicken stock

Coq au Vin with Herby Dumplings

In a classic Coq au Vin, the French would not dream of serving dumplings but, as I am not French, I don't care!

Serves 4

2 tbsp olive oil

8 skinless, boneless chicken thighs, halved

16 button mushrooms

4 rashers smoked streaky bacon, cut into lardons

2 banana shallots, finely sliced

1 large carrot, finely diced

3 garlic cloves, chopped

1 tbsp plain white flour

1 tbsp tomato purée

600ml (1 pint) red wine

300ml (½ pint) chicken stock

bouquet garni (2 bay leaves, fresh thyme and parsley sprigs, tied with kitchen string)

sea salt and freshly ground black pepper

for the dumplings

100g (4oz) self-raising flour

½ tsp salt

1½ tsp olive oil

a small handful fresh parsley, chopped

3 tsp snipped fresh chives

60ml (2½ fl oz) semi-skimmed milk

Step one Preheat the oven to 180°C/350°F/gas 4. Add 1 tablespoon of oil to a large, heavy-based, lidded casserole over medium heat. Season the chicken thighs with salt and pepper. Brown in the oil in two batches for 4 minutes on each side, then transfer to a plate and set aside. Add the mushrooms and cook for 5 minutes or until golden. (If the pan appears dry, add a little boiling water and scrape the bottom to pick up any chickeny residue.) Set the mushrooms aside with the chicken.

Step two Add the remaining tablespoon of oil to the pan, then add the bacon and fry over a high heat for 2 minutes. Reduce the heat and add the shallots and carrot. Cover the pan and sweat the vegetables over a low heat for 10 minutes, adding the garlic for the last minute.

Step three Add the plain flour and tomato purée and stir, coating the vegetables, for 1 minute. Gradually pour in the wine, stirring as you go to emulsify the sauce. Add the stock, chicken, mushrooms and bouquet garni and stir through. Cover and bake for 1 hour, stirring halfway through the cooking time.

Step four To make the dumplings, mix all the ingredients together and shape into 8 small balls. For the last 20 minutes of the casserole cooking time, add the dumplings and cover. They will double in size during cooking. Remove the lid for the last 5 minutes' cooking time so that they become golden on top. Remove the bouquet garni before serving.

Moroccan Chicken Couscous

A proper couscous is served with a brothy, Moroccan-spiced stew.

Step one Heat the oil in a large heavy-bottomed pan. Add the chicken pieces and cook until brown all over. You may need to do this in batches. Remove the chicken with a slotted spoon and set aside. Add the onions to the pan and cook for 5 minutes, or until they have softened and started to go golden. Make sure you really scrape away at the chicken residue at the bottom of the pan. Add the garlic and chillies for the last minute of cooking.

Step two Add 1 teaspoon salt, ½ teaspoon black pepper, the rest of the spices, the bay leaves and thyme sprigs and cook for 1 minute. Pour over the stock, then return the chicken to the pan along with the turnips, carrots and courgettes. Cook on a lowish heat for 40 minutes – the chicken should be melting off the bones. Drain and rinse the chickpeas and add them for the last 10 minutes of cooking.

Step three Meanwhile, put the couscous into a large mixing bowl, add some salt and pour over enough boiling water to cover it by 5mm (¼in). Cover and leave for 10 minutes to absorb the water, then uncover and fluff up the grains with a fork. Dress with the olive oil and lemon juice and stir in the chopped coriander. Serve the chicken stew on top of the couscous, with a good dollop of harissa alongside.

Serves 4

3 tbsp vegetable oil

1 chicken, cut into 8 pieces

2 large onions, cut into eighths

4 garlic cloves, chopped

2 green chillies, seeded and chopped

½ tsp cayenne pepper

1 tsp ground cumin

1 tsp paprika

2 bay leaves

a few fresh thyme sprigs

900ml (1½ pints) chicken stock

2 turnips, quartered

4 carrots, cut into thirds

2 large courgettes, halved lengthways and each half cut into thirds

400g (14oz) tin chickpeas

sea salt and freshly ground black pepper

for the couscous

300g (10½ oz) couscous

2 tbsp extra virgin olive oil

juice of ½ lemon

a small bunch fresh coriander, chopped

harissa, to serve

Sticky Barbecue Chicken Wings with Blue Cheese Dressing and Celery

There is no denying that nibbling on chicken wings and getting spicy, sticky barbecue sauce all over your fingers and face is one of life's great pleasures. These wings are just as delicious served straight from the oven as they are cold.

Makes 40 pieces

20 chicken wings

2 tbsp olive oil

sea salt and freshly ground black pepper

for the barbecue sauce

150ml (¼ pint) tomato ketchup

120ml (4fl oz) cider vinegar

4 tbsp soft dark brown sugar

2 tbsp hot sauce, such as chipotle Tabasco

1 tsp ground cumin

1 tsp smoked paprika

for the blue cheese dressing

100g (4oz) blue cheese, preferably Gorgonzola

200ml (7fl oz) soured cream

a squeeze of lemon juice

4 celery sticks, quartered lengthways, to serve

Step one Preheat the oven to 220°C/425°F/gas 7. To prepare the chicken, cut through the joint of each wing, keeping the two meaty pieces and discarding the tip. Set the chicken pieces on a large baking tray, drizzle with olive oil and sprinkle with salt and pepper. Roast for 20 minutes, then reduce the temperature to 180°C/350°F/gas 4 and cook for a further 10 minutes.

Step two Meanwhile, put all of the barbecue ingredients together in a pan over medium heat and let it bubble away for 3–5 minutes to thicken up a little. Taste and add more seasoning if necessary. Remove from the heat and reserve until needed.

Step three Remove chicken from the oven and cover the wings in half of the barbecue sauce. Return to the oven for another 30 minutes.

Step four Meanwhile, mash together all the ingredients for the blue cheese dressing, retaining a few lumps. When the chicken wings are cooked, pour the remaining sauce over them and toss so that they become sticky. Serve the wings with the celery sticks and the blue cheese dressing.

Griddled White-Pepper-Crusted Guinea Fowl with Green Apple Salad

Guinea fowl has more flavour than chicken, is simple to cook and is becoming really easy to get hold of and more affordable.

Step one Place the guinea fowl pieces into a bowl and set aside. Add the lemongrass, ginger, garlic, white pepper, 1 teaspoon of the sea salt and the oil to a food-processor and whizz until it becomes a paste. Rub the paste all over the guinea fowl. Cover and leave to marinate for at least 2 hours or overnight.

Step two When you are ready to cook preheat the oven to 180°C/350°F/gas 4 and heat a griddle pan until almost smoking. Set the guinea fowl pieces on the griddle and cook for 4 minutes on each side, or until golden and slightly charred. Place on a baking sheet and roast for 15 minutes, then remove from the oven and leave to rest for 5 minutes.

Step three To make the dressing, whizz together the garlic, chilli and sugar in a food-processor to make a rough paste. Stir in the fish sauce and lime juice, and season to taste.

Step four To make the salad, fry the shallots in the oil for 5 minutes, or until crisp and golden brown. Remove with a slotted spoon and drain on kitchen paper. Toss the apples in a bowl with the lime juice and add the tomatoes and dressing.

Step five Spoon the salad onto plates and top with the crisp shallots and coriander. Slice the guinea fowl into 1cm/½in-thick slices, add them to the plates and serve.

Serves 2

1 guinea fowl, boned and quartered (ask your butcher to do this)

2 stalks of lemongrass, outer leaves discarded, stems roughly chopped

2.5cm (1in) piece fresh root ginger, peeled and roughly chopped

3 garlic cloves, peeled

1 tsp white pepper

2 tbsp groundnut or vegetable oil

sea salt and freshly ground black pepper

for the dressing

1 garlic clove, chopped

1 red chilli, seeded and finely chopped

1 tsp golden caster sugar

1 tbsp Thai fish sauce

juice of 2 limes

for the salad

3 shallots, finely sliced

1 tbsp vegetable oil

4 sharp, green apples, cored and thinly sliced

1 tbsp lime juice

6 cherry tomatoes, quartered

a handful of coriander, finely chopped

Pan-fried Duck Breast with Pitta, Soured Cream and Salad

They do a pretty mean duck dish in Eastern Europe using cream and cucumber. Not great for the ticker, but delicious all the same.

Serves 4

4 pitta breads

olive oil

4 duck breasts, skin on

sea salt and freshly ground black pepper

for the salad

1 cucumber, peeled, cut in half lengthways, seeded and thinly sliced into half-moons

¼ tsp salt

280ml (9fl oz) soured cream

1 small bunch of fresh dill, finely chopped

a pinch of smoked paprika, plus extra to sprinkle

Step one Heat a frying pan until very hot. Place the duck breasts in the pan, skin-side down. Reduce the heat to medium and pan-fry for 8 minutes or until the fat has rendered from the duck and into the pan and the skin has turned golden and crisp. Turn the duck breasts over and cook on the other side for 4 minutes to give a perfect pink colour. Remove the duck breasts from the pan and leave to rest, uncovered so that the skin stays crisp, for 5 minutes. Meanwhile pour the fat out of the pan but reserve the pan juices. Slice the duck breasts into thin slices.

Step two To make the salad, simply mix together the cucumber and salt and leave to drain for 10 minutes in a sieve. Mix the drained cucumber with the soured cream, dill and paprika and season with some black pepper.

Step three Warm the pitta breads in the oven and serve each duck breast on a disc of grilled bread, with some salad alongside. Pour over the juices from the duck, then drizzle with olive oil and sprinkle with a spot more paprika.

To really impress, why not try serving this with pomegranate molasses drizzled over and sprinkled with pomegranate seeds.

Roast Chicken with Truffle Gnocchi, Sage Butter and Cavolo Nero

It may sounds tricky, but in fact making gnocchi is as easy as making a scone. Truffle paste may sound like an indulgent ingredient, but a little goes a long way and it's a super store-cupboard ingredient to really jazz up your dinners.

Step one Heat the oven to 220°C/425°F/gas 7. Mix the butter with the sage leaves and rub it under the skin of the chicken. Season the chicken lightly with salt. Roast for 20 minutes, then reduce the heat to 180°C/350°F/gas 4 and cook for 1 hour or until the juices run clear when the thickest part is pierced with a skewer Remove from the oven and leave to rest.

Step two To make the gnocchi, carefully scoop out the flesh of the baked potatoes and mash in a large bowl. Form in a well in the centre and add the flour, salt and Parmesan. Mix well, then slowly add in the truffle paste and beaten egg yolk. With clean, floured hands, press the mixture together to form dough. Add a little flour if the mixture is too wet. Do not overwork it. Tip the dough on to a floured surface and roll it into a long sausage. Cut it into 2.5cm (1in) lengths and press down the tops with a fork, then gently press the sides so the gnocchi resemble pillows.

Step three To make the sage and truffle sauce, put the 25g (1oz) butter and whole sage leaves in a small pan over a medium heat. Let the butter cook until it is golden brown and smells nutty. Remove from the heat and stir in the truffle oil.

Step four Bring a pan of salted water to the boil, then poach the gnocchi and cavolo nero for 1–2 minutes or until the gnocchi rise to the surface. Strain away the water then stir in the sauce to coat. Cook until the gnocchi are catching in places. Transfer to a serving dish. Carve or portion the chicken, then place on top of the gnocchi. Drizzle over the chicken juices and any leftover butter sage and truffle sauce.

Serves 4

1 tbsp butter

3 sage leaves, chopped

1 medium chicken

250g (9oz) evenly sized floury potatoes, baked and still hot

50g (2oz) Italian '00' flour or plain flour, plus extra for dusting

25g (1oz) finely grated Parmesan cheese, plus extra for serving

½ tsp white truffle paste or white truffle oil

1 egg yolk, lightly beaten

60g (2½ oz) cavolo nero, or any cabbage in season, shredded

sea salt

for the sage and truffle sauce

25g (1oz) unsalted butter

4 large sage leaves

1–2 tsp truffle-infused olive oil

Jamaican Brown Chicken Stew

I first got introduced to Caribbean food when I was working as a body piercer in Camden as there was an abundance of small but excellent Caribbean restaurants and takeaways in the area at the time. This classic brown chicken stew has to be one of my favourites.

Serves 4

1 medium chicken, cut into 8 portions

1 tsp sea salt

1 tsp vegetable oil

3 spring onions, chopped

2 onions, chopped

1 Scotch bonnet chilli pepper, seeded and chopped

a few thyme sprigs

4 cloves garlic, chopped

2 tbsp curry powder

pinch allspice mix

½ red peppers, seeded, chopped

½ green pepper, seeded and chopped

600ml (1 pint) chicken stock, fresh is best

225g (8oz) butternut squash, peeled and cut into bite-sized cubes

200g (7oz) potatoes, peeled and cut into bite sized cubes

to serve

550g (1¼ lb) Basmati rice, cooked in coconut milk

Step one Heat the vegetable oil in a large, deep flameproof casserole or sauté pan with a lid until really hot. Add 4–5 pieces of chicken to the oil and fry gently skin-side down for about 5 minutes on each side until the chicken is browned all over.

Step two Remove the chicken from the casserole and repeat with the remaining chicken pieces. Carefully pour out most of the oil, leaving just 2 spoonfuls in the base. Add the spring onions, onions, chilli, garlic, thyme and peppers, and stir briefly. Return the chicken to the casserole with the spices, the squash and potatoes. Pour in the stock, then add the butter, bring to the boil and then reduce the heat, cover and simmer for 25 minutes until the liquid is reduced to a rich gravy and the chicken is cooked through. Serve with the coconut rice.

KITCHEN TABLE

For a video masterclass on how to tell if your chicken is cooked, go to www.mykitchentable.co.uk/videos/cookingchicken

Grilled Curried Chicken with Rice, Lentil and Courgette Salad

A super-healthy weeknight supper that is crammed full of different textures and flavours. It's cheap, it's quick, it's delicious and it's healthy. What more could you want from a meal?

Step one Cover the lentils in unsalted water (salt tends to toughen lentils) and bring to the boil. Reduce to a simmer and cook on a low heat for 20 minutes or until tender. Meanwhile, in a separate pan cover the Basmati rice with enough water so that it comes about 1cm (½in) above the level of the rice. Soak for 5 minutes. Cover and bring to the boil. Once almost all the water has been absorbed, turn off the heat and leave covered for a further 5 minutes.

Step two Toss the chicken with 1 teaspoon of the olive oil, then the curry powder and some sea salt. Toss the courgette strips with the remaining teaspoon olive oil and the garlic, and season. Place a griddle over a high heat until it begins to smoke. Griddle the chicken thighs for 5 minutes on each side or until a little charred and cooked through. Transfer to a plate and keep warm while you griddle the courgettes for a minute or two on each side until lightly charred.

Step three Drain the lentils and toss them with the rice, charred courgette, coriander and lemon juice. Mix the yoghurt with the mint sauce. Slice the chicken and serve on top of the lentil salad, with a dollop of the yoghurt dressing.

Serves 4

100g (4oz) green or Puy lentils

150g (5oz) Basmati rice

4 boneless chicken thighs (I prefer the skin left on)

2 tsp olive oil

2 tsp madras curry powder

2 courgettes, sliced lengthways into thin strips

1 garlic clove, crushed

½ small bunch fresh coriander, chopped

juice of ½ lemon

75ml (2½ fl oz) natural yoghurt

1 tsp mint sauce, or ½ small bunch fresh mint, stems discarded, leaves chopped

sea salt and freshly ground black pepper

Chicken in Weeds

Don't be put off by the name – it's not really cooked in weeds, just tons of coriander, which is used almost as a vegetable. I can't take credit for this recipe, it's one of my mum's, and she honed it from a Madhur Jaffrey recipe many moons ago. We were brought up on this stuff, as it's so mild that it's great for kids. It's tinged with lemon and ginger, which make it quite user-friendly. When asked what we wanted for dinner as kids you could bet your bottom dollar you'd hear me and my sisters screaming in unison, 'Chicken in weeds!'

Serves 4

5cm (2in) piece fresh root ginger, peeled and chopped

300ml (½ pint) water or chicken stock, plus 4 tbsp

4 tbsp vegetable oil

8 skinless chicken thighs, bone in

1 onion, finely chopped

5 garlic cloves, finely chopped

200g (7oz) finely chopped fresh coriander

1 long green chilli, seeded and finely chopped

½ tsp cayenne pepper

2 tsp ground cumin

1 tsp ground coriander

½ tsp ground turmeric

sea salt

2 tbsp lemon juice

Step one Put the ginger and the 4 tablespoons of water or chicken stock into a food-processor and blitz to a paste. Heat the oil to a large heavy-based pan placed over a medium heat. Add the chicken thighs in batches and brown. Scoop the chicken out with a slotted spoon and leave to rest on a plate while you cook the next batch.

Step two Add the onion to the pan and cook on a low heat for about 10 minutes, or until softened and turning golden. Add the garlic for the last few minutes of cooking. Pour over the ginger paste and stir-fry until starting to brown. Add the chopped fresh coriander, chilli, all the spices and some salt and cook for a further minute.

Step three Return the chicken to the pan, along with any juices from the plate. Add the water or stock and the lemon juice, cover the pan and cook for 15 minutes. Turn the chicken over, then put the lid back on and cook for a further 15 minutes. If the sauce is too thin, cook with the lid off until it's thickened up a bit. The chicken should be falling off of the bone when it's ready. Serve with rice.

Thai Green Curry – The Genuine Article

My obsession with authenticity is going to have you making a trip to an Asian supermarket. However, peas, beans and asparagus work well too.

Step one Put all the paste ingredients into a blender and blitz until smooth. Pick the spring pea aubergines off of their stems and halve the green aubergines and set aside.

Step two Heat a large wok or pan, add the paste and stir-fry for 1 minute, or until the room fills with a gorgeous aroma.

Step three Add the chicken and all the prepared aubergines to the paste. Pour over the coconut milk and add the fish sauce. Stir in the palm sugar, lime leaves and chilli. Simmer for about 7 minutes, or until the chicken and aubergines are cooked through and the sauce has thickened a little. Pour into a serving dish and swirl in the coconut cream. Sprinkle over the Thai basil leaves. Serve with rice.

To make prawn Thai green curry, replace the chicken with 24 raw, peeled king prawns. For vegetarian Thai green curry, replace the chicken with 200g (7oz) cubed firm tofu, 100g (4oz) broccoli florets and 12 cobs of baby corn.

Serves 4

2 handfuls spring pea aubergines

8 green aubergines

4 boneless chicken breasts

2 x 400g (14oz) tins coconut milk

2 tbsp Thai fish sauce

1 tbsp palm sugar

2 lime leaves, sliced

1 red chilli, seeded and sliced

1 x 100g (4oz) carton coconut cream

a few Thai basil leaves

for the paste

2 long green chillies

10 green bird's-eye chilllies

1 tbsp chopped lemongrass

3 shallots, chopped

8 garlic cloves, chopped

a small bunch fresh coriander

½ tsp ground cumin

2 tsp ground coriander

½ tsp white pepper

3 lime leaves, chopped

2 tsp shrimp paste

1 tsp salt

3 tbsp groundnut or vegetable oil

Sunny's (Legendary) Chicken Curry

Sunny is my pal. She's British but her family hails from the Punjab, in northern India. I once asked her what the trick was to curry-making and she said it's just about giving the curry some love, and letting it have the time it needs during cooking for all the flavours to develop.

Serves 4

2 tbsp ghee or butter

2–3 large onions, chopped

1 tbsp cumin seeds

4–6 garlic cloves, crushed

2.5cm (1in) piece fresh root ginger, peeled and grated

1–2 long green chillies, seeded and finely chopped

1 tbsp ground turmeric

1 tbsp garam masala

1 tbsp ground coriander

1 tsp chilli powder

1 tsp Madras curry powder

200g (7oz) tinned chopped tomatoes

8 skinless chicken thighs, bone in

500ml (17fl oz) chicken stock or water

a generous handful fresh coriander, chopped

sea salt and freshly ground black pepper

Step one Put a full kettle on to boil. Heat the ghee or butter in a large deep pan with a lid. Add the onions and sauté for about 5 minutes until slightly golden, then add some salt and the cumin seeds and sauté for a further 2 minutes. Add the garlic, ginger and chillies and cook for a further 3 minutes, until everything is nicely golden.

Step two Increase the heat and add enough boiling water to just cover the onions. Simmer gently, stirring occasionally, until the water has reduced almost completely (be careful not to let the onions burn). Keep adding water for 10–15 minutes, or until the onions are mushy. You are looking to make this into a paste, so by all means go at it with a potato masher.

Step three Reduce the heat to medium, add some more boiling water (again just covering the paste), then stir in the spices. Cover the pan (as it starts to splatter in all directions) and simmer for about 5–10 minutes. Add the tomatoes. At this stage, it should be quite soupy, so if it's too watery, keep simmering it until it has reduced.

Step four Add the chicken and give everything a good stir. Pour over the stock or water, making sure there is enough to just cover the chicken. Leave to simmer on a low heat, stirring it every now and then, for 40 minutes. Stir in the coriander, check the seasoning and serve. In the words of Sunny: "Job done!"

Afghan Yoghurt Chicken

The Afghan Kitchen restaurant in Islington, north London, sells one of the best curries in London. A simple yoghurt and chicken curry, the recipe has been a carefully guarded secret of theirs for many years. Their tight-lipped silence only made me more curious, so I put my conjuring gloves on and here, after years of refining, is my version. I hope you'll agree I've done a good job.

Step one Add the oil to a medium-sized casserole with a lid over a medium heat. Brown the chicken in batches. Transfer to a plate using a slotted spoon and set aside. Reduce the heat to low and add the onion to the fat remaining in the pan. Cook for 8 minutes, or until the onion has softened and taken on a lightly caramelised tinge. For the last minute of cooking add the garlic and chilli.

Step two Add the spices and cook for 1 minute. Add the yoghurt, the browned chicken with all its juices and a splash of water. Give it a good stir and add the chopped herbs and a little salt and pepper. Stir again, then cover with a lid and let it poach away for 20 minutes. The trick to this curry is slow cooking, so just let it bubble gently. The curry is ready when the chicken is cooked through and tender and the sauce has thickened. Don't be worried if the sauce looks a little curdled – it's caused by the yoghurt, but you can stir in a splash of water if you like to even it out. Serve with rice.

Serves 4

1 tbsp groundnut or vegetable oil

8 boneless chicken thighs, skin removed, each cut into 4 pieces

1 onion, finely chopped

5 garlic cloves, chopped

1 green chilli, seeded and finely chopped

1 tsp ground coriander

1 tsp ground cumin

3 cardamom pods, crushed

1 tsp hot paprika

450g (1lb) Greek yoghurt

a small bunch fresh coriander, stems discarded, leaves finely chopped

a small bunch fresh mint, stems discarded, leaves finely chopped

sea salt and freshly ground black pepper

Chicken Katsu Curry

Anyone who is into Japanese food knows that katsu curry is wickedly wonderful. What makes it stand out from other curries is that the meat is breaded and fried before being slathered in a luxurious silky curry sauce. I've used chicken here, but I have also eaten this made with juicy king prawns or pork tenderloin, both equally delicious. Offering crunch, spice and sauce, this is real comfort food.

Serves 4

100g (4oz) plain flour

sea salt and freshly ground black pepper

1 egg, lightly beaten

200g (7oz) Japanese panko breadcrumbs

4 boneless, skinless chicken breasts

100ml (4fl oz) groundnut or vegetable oil

for the curry sauce

1 tbsp groundnut or vegetable oil

1 onion, chopped

5 garlic cloves

2 carrots, chopped

2 tbsp plain flour

1 tbsp medium curry powder

600ml (1 pint) chicken stock

2 tsp honey

1 tbsp soy sauce

1 bay leaf

⅛ tsp garam masala

to serve

hot steamed rice

salad

Step one To make the sauce, heat the tablespoon of oil in a pan. Add the onion and garlic and sauté for 2 minutes, then stir in the carrots. Cover and and cook gently for 10 minutes, stirring occasionally until the vegetables soften and start to caramelise.

Step two Stir in the flour and curry powder. Cook for 1 minute. Slowly pour in the stock, stirring until combined to avoid getting lumps. Stir in the honey, soy sauce and bay leaf and bring to the boil, then reduce the heat to a slow simmer and cook for 20 minutes. The sauce will have thickened and taken on all of the flavours, although it still needs to have a pouring consistency. Add the garam masala, then pass the sauce through a sieve. (I prefer it nice and smooth but some people might like a chunky sauce, so feel free not to strain it.)

Step three To prepare the chicken, season the flour with lots of salt and pepper. Place the seasoned flour, egg and breadcrumbs on separate plates. Coat the chicken first in the flour, then in the egg and finally into the breadcrumbs.

Step four Heat the 100ml (4fl oz) oil in a frying pan and fry the breaded chicken breasts for 5 minutes on each side, or until golden and cooked through. Remove from the pan with a slotted spoon and leave to drain on kitchen paper. Slice the chicken on the diagonal and serve over rice with the sauce drizzled on top, and a salad alongside.

For a really authentic katsu curry, serve it with Japanese pickles.

Chicken, Leek and Ham Pies

My younger sister, Cora, is a chicken-pie connoisseur. I am not sure if it is possible for her to turn down a chicken pie if it is on the menu, and it was the first recipe she asked my advice on. This recipe is special to me, as it is something we have honed together – a real Erskine special – and I hope you get as much pleasure out of it as we have.

Step one Melt the butter in a medium-sized pan over a low heat, add the leeks and cook for 10 minutes, or until softened. For the last minute of cooking time, add the garlic.

Step two Stir in the flour and cook for a minute, then add the white wine, chicken stock and cream and simmer for 1 minute. Add the chicken and ham and simmer for 5 minutes, until the chicken is just cooked through but not over-cooked, and the sauce has thickened. Stir in the thyme and parsley and season to taste.

Step three Divide the chicken mixture between 4 individual pie dishes and leave to cool for 10 minutes. Meanwhile, preheat the oven to 200°C/400°F/gas 6, and dust a work surface with flour and roll out the pastry. Cut out 4 pastry lids big enough to cover each pie dish. Using a pastry brush, brush egg yolk round the edge of each pie dish and top with a pastry lid. Pierce each lid with a skewer and brush more egg yolk all over the lids. Chill in the fridge for 10 minutes (or all day if you like).

Step four Bake the pies for 20 minutes, or until the pastry is cooked through and lovely and crisp and the chicken is bubbling away inside.

Serves 4

2 tbsp butter

3 leeks, finely sliced

3 garlic cloves, finely chopped

2 tbsp plain flour, plus extra for dusting

100ml (4fl oz) white wine

400ml (14fl oz) chicken stock

50ml (2fl oz) double cream

2 chicken breasts, chopped into bite-sized pieces

200g (7oz) cooked ham ends (from the deli counter)

a few fresh thyme sprigs, leaves picked

1 tbsp chopped fresh parsley

1 x 500g backet of all-butter puff pastry

1 large egg yolk

sea salt and freshly ground black pepper

Chateaubriand of Tuna with Tomato Hollandaise and Zucchini Fritti

There is nothing sexier than sharing your food and bringing a whole piece of fish or meat to the table to carve has a real wow factor.

Serves 2

300g (11 oz) freshest tuna loin, in one large even piece

sea salt and freshly ground black pepper

1 tsp fennel seeds

1 tsp coriander seeds

¼ tsp dried red chilli flakes

1 tbsp olive oil

for the tomato hollandaise sauce

1½ tbsp cider vinegar

1 mandarin orange, juiced

2 large free-range egg yolks

150g (5oz) butter, melted and still hot

1 tomato, seeded and chopped

1 tsp chopped fresh chervil

for the zucchini fritti

200ml (7 fl oz) olive or vegetable oil

100g (4oz) plain flour

1 tsp sea salt

½ tsp white pepper

3 green courgettes, cut into thin matchsticks

Step one Preheat the oven to 200°C/400°F/gas 6. Lay the tuna on a board and season with salt and pepper. Place the spices in a pestle and mortar or a coffee grinder and grind until broken up. Mix the spices in a bowl with the olive oil, then rub the spice mix all over the tuna to form a crust. Heat an ovenproof roasting pan on the hob and brown the tuna for 1 minute on each side. Finish in the oven for 5 minutes, then remove and leave to rest, covered, for 5 minutes.

Step two To make the tomato hollandaise, place the vinegar and mandarin juice in a pan and bring to the boil. Reduce until there is just 1 or 2 teaspoons of liquid left in the pan, then pour into a food processor. Add the egg yolks and start to whizz. Very, very slowly add the hot melted butter, dribble by dribble. The dressing will become quite thick if you are patient. This whole process can take as long as 10 minutes, so you really must do it as slowly as you can.

Step three To make the zucchini fritti, pour enough oil into a deep but narrow pan to come one-third of the way up the sides, and heat it until hot enough to fry in (a good way of testing this is to drop a small piece of bread into the oil; if it turns golden brown in 20–25 seconds the oil is ready – any faster and it is too hot; any slower and it's not hot enough). Mix the flour, salt and white pepper together. Coat the courgette matchsticks in the flour mixture, dust them off a little and drop half of them into the oil. Deep-fry for 30–40 seconds, turning once, then remove, drain on kitchen paper and repeat with the other half.

Step four To serve, lay the tuna on a chopping board, place the courgettes in a pile next to the tuna and pour the hollandaise into a small bowl.

Batters

Here are two batters for some tasty deep-fried fish. The tempura works fantastically well with prawns, fish and vegetables; while the marriage of beer batter and light white fish is something that every Brit should be truly proud of. Both recipes make 300ml (½ pint) of batter.

Step one When making these batters, mix all the ingredients together in a bowl. For the tempura batter, do not over-mix the ingredients – it is better that this batter is a bit lumpy than over mixed and totally smooth. You also need to ensure that the water is ice-cold for the tempura batter. Add some ice cubes if you're worried it's not cold enough. For the beer batter, however, you need to beat all the ingredients together until the mixture becomes a smooth batter that's free from lumps.

Step two Pour enough light vegetable, sunflower or corn oil into either a deep-fat fryer or a large saucepan so it comes one third of the way up the pan. You ideally need a pan that is deep enough to deal with 8cm (3¼in) of oil. Heat the oil to 190°C/375°F. You can test that the oil is ready by dropping in a piece of bread – it should brown in 20 seconds.

Step three Dip the fish or vegetables into the batter, shaking off any excess, and fry until golden and crisp. Fry in small batches, and remove each batch as you go with a slotted spoon to drain on kitchen paper. To keep things crisp and warm while you are frying, heat the oven to 150°C/300°F/gas 2 and line a baking sheet with greaseproof paper. Place each batch on the baking sheet after it's been cooked to keep it warm in the oven, but leave the door open to keep it crisp.

Tempura Batter

85g (3½oz) plain flour

1 tbsp cornflour

½ tsp sea salt

200ml (7fl oz) ice-cold sparkling water

oil for frying

Beer Batter

100g (4oz) self-raising flour

½ tsp salt

150ml (¼ pint) ice-cold beer or ale

oil for frying

Pan-fried Plaice with Prawn, Lime and Chilli Butter

I've always found the delicate flakiness of plaice to be such a treat that it seems a shame we are more often drawn to the more obvious charms of salmon and cod. It's one of the easiest fish to work with and tastes marvellous. I came across a similar dish to this while on holiday in Cornwall, and was so inspired – fantastic fish and the best of British produce, with the flavours of Thailand running through it.

Serves 4

4 plaice fillets, skin on

50g (2oz) plain flour, seasoned with salt and pepper

2 tbsp olive oil

80g (3¼ oz) butter, plus 1 tbsp

3 garlic cloves, finely chopped

1 red chilli, seeded and finely chopped

200g (7oz) small cooked peeled prawns

a small bunch of fresh coriander, finely chopped

juice of 1 lime

sea salt and freshly ground black pepper

Step one Toss the plaice fillets in enough seasoned flour to coat them evenly but thinly. Heat the oil in a frying pan and add the tablespoon of butter. When it starts to foam, lay the fish fillets in the pan, skin-side down. Pan-fry for 2–3 minutes on each side, or until the fish is crisp and golden on the outside, but nicely opaque in the middle (you may need to do this in two batches). Remove from the pan and place on a piece of kitchen paper to drain.

Step two Tip out the oil, wipe the pan with a piece of kitchen paper, then add the 80g (3¼ oz) of butter. Once it starts to foam, tip in the garlic and chilli and sauté for 1 minute or until the garlic is cooked. Add the prawns and fry for a further minute. Finally add the coriander, lime juice and seasoning. Lay a plaice fillet on each plate and cover with a couple of spoonfuls of the prawn and butter sauce.

Five-spice Salted Chilli Squid

I can't go into a Vietnamese restaurant without ordering crispy salted chilli squid, which knocks spots off regular calamari. I learned the little trick of adding Chinese five-spice powder from a chef on London's Kingsland Road, a prominent Vietnamese area. Five spice isn't traditional, but it does make it really aromatic and gives it a sweeter finish.

Step one In a large bowl, combine the flour, cornflour, Chinese five-spice, chilli powder and salt. Add the squid rings and tentacles, and toss to coat, shaking off any excess flour.

Step two Heat the oil in a large pan or wok big enough to deep-fry in. Add half the squid and deep-fry for about 1 minute, or until just tender and beginning to colour. Remove with a slotted spoon and drain well on kitchen paper. Repeat the process with the remaining squid.

Step three In a wok or frying pan, heat another tablespoon of oil. Add the garlic and fry for about 30 seconds, then add the chilli and fry for a further 30 seconds. Finally, add the spring onions and fry for 30 seconds. Remove with a slotted spoon. Arrange the squid on a platter and garnish with the fried garlic, chillies and spring onions. Serve immediately with lemon wedges.

Serves 4

50g (2oz) plain flour

1 tbsp cornflour

1 tsp Chinese five-spice powder

1 tsp hot chilli powder

1 tbsp sea salt

600g (1¼ lb) whole squid, cleaned and prepared, bodies cut into rings (see page 51)

vegetable oil, for deep-frying

3 garlic cloves, finely chopped

2 large red chillies, cut into rings

2 tbsp sliced spring onion

lemon wedges, to serve

Grilled Fish with Chilli and Mango Sauce

For those of you who have been to Thailand, or any part of South-east Asia for that matter, and spent time at beach restaurants, this is a dish that will bring back a flood of memories. If you want it hotter add more chilli, a bit sweeter add more sugar. If you're squeamish you can swap the whole fish for fish fillets. I've gone for sea bass, but the sauce works beautifully with any fish really.

Serves 2

1 medium-sized sea bass, snapper or grey mullet, gutted and scaled

2 tbsp Thai fish sauce

3 tbsp Shaohsing wine or sherry

3 garlic cloves, finely chopped

a handful of fresh coriander, chopped

2 tbsp soy sauce

juice of 2 limes

1 fresh red chilli, seeded and chopped

½ firm mango (green, under-ripe mangoes are great if you can find them), peeled and cut into matchsticks

200ml (7fl oz) water

1 tsp tamarind paste

2 tsp brown sugar

1 tsp cornflour, mixed with 2 tbsp water

a handful of coriander leaves, to garnish

hot steamed rice and pak choy, to serve

Step one Preheat the grill to high. Using a sharp serrated knife, and holding the fish firmly in front of you, make 3–4 cuts on each side. This allows the marinade and sauce to penetrate. Put the fish into a bowl, pour the fish sauce over and leave to marinate for 5–10 minutes.

Step two Put all the remaining ingredients except the cornflour mixture and the coriander into a saucepan. Place over a medium heat and bring gently to a simmer. Pour in the cornflour mixture and stir until thickened. Keep the pan on minimum heat until you have cooked the fish, or cover and keep warm.

Step three Grill the fish for 8 minutes on each side or until crisp and golden on the outside but firm and flaky when pushed in its meatiest part. Place on a serving platter and pour over the sauce. Sprinkle with the coriander and serve with steamed rice and pak choi.

Korean Seafood Pancakes

My favourite secret haunt in London is a Korean restaurant called Dotori in Finsbury Park. The seafood pancakes are tremendous and inspired me to make my own. They are light and crisp and make the most wonderful throw together meal if you're tired after work.

Step one For the dipping sauce, mix the rice wine vinegar, soy sauce, honey and sesame oil together and place to one side in a dipping bowl.

Step two Next, make the pancakes. Mix the seafood, onions, courgette, mirin, flour, water and eggs in a large bowl.

Step three Heat the oil in a frying pan and add the batter. Once golden on the bottom, flip over and cook the other side. Once both sides are golden brown, cut into eight triangles or fry individual American-style size pancakes.

Step four Quickly fry the shiitake mushrooms and serve scattered over the pancakes with the dipping sauce.

Serves 4

for the pancakes

15 raw prawns, peeled

1 whole squid, cleaned and prepared, body cut into rings (see page 51)

150g (5 oz) crab meat

10 spring onions, cut into 3cm (1¼ in) strips

175g (6oz) courgettes, grated

1 tsp mirin

100g (4oz) plain flour

50ml (2fl oz) iced fizzy water

2 medium free-range eggs

1 tbsp oil

250g (9oz) shiitake mushrooms, cut into quarters

for the dipping sauce

1 tbsp rice wine vinegar

1 tbsp soy sauce

½ tsp clear honey

½ tsp sesame oil

Vietnamese Prawns and Lemongrass

The minuscule amount of preparation needed for this dish is worth every second as it is so quick to cook. This is fast food at its best and most authentic. Fat juicy prawns with a heady lemongrass sauce – truly too good to be believed, and made in less time and with less money than it would take to order it from a takeaway, to boot. Quite possibly the easiest yet most impressive recipe in this book!

Serves 2

1 tbsp groundnut oil

1 small onion, cut into slivers

2 spring onions, cut into 2.5cm (1in) pieces

12 large prawns, shelled and deveined

juice of 2 lemons

4 tbsp Thai fish sauce

½ tsp chilli powder

2 tsp brown sugar

4 tbsp chicken stock

2 lime leaves, thinly sliced

2 shallots, finely chopped

1 stalk of lemongrass, finely chopped

hot steamed rice and Oriental greens, to serve

Step one Heat the oil in a wok or frying pan until it is smoking, then add the onion, spring onions and prawns. Stir-fry for 2 minutes, or until the prawns start to curl up and get a bit of colour on them. Add all the remaining ingredients and bring to the boil for 1 minute. That's it! Serve with steamed rice and Oriental greens.

Nasi Goreng

This dish is more special than any other fried rice I can think of because it has so many different textures and flavours.

Step one Preheat the grill to high. Put all the nasi goreng paste ingredients into a food-processor and blend until smooth. Slice the mackerel in half, crossways and season on both sides with salt and pepper. Lay the fish on a lightly oiled baking tray or the rack of a grill pan, and grill for 4 minutes on each side.

Step two Pour the sunflower oil into a wok. Add the shallots and fry over a medium heat until crisp and golden brown. Lift them out with a slotted spoon and leave to drain on kitchen paper. Add 2 tablespoons of the nasi goreng paste and stir-fry for 2 minutes. Add the chicken and prawns and stir-fry for 5 minutes or until golden brown.

Step three Add the cooked rice and stir-fry over a high heat for 2 minutes until heated through. Add the fried shallots and stir-fry for a further minute. Add the soy sauce and most of the spring onions, then toss together well and divide between serving plates.

Step four Fry the eggs in a frying pan. Serve each portion of nasi goreng with a fried egg, a piece of mackerel and some cucumber slices, and sprinkle with the remaining spring onions.

Serves 4

2 mackerel fillets

4 tbsp sunflower oil

6 large shallots, sliced

1 boneless chicken breast, thinly sliced

200g (7oz) small cooked prawns

250g (9oz) basmati rice, cooked and cooled

1 tbsp light soy sauce

4 spring onions, sliced

4 large eggs

5cm (2in) piece of cucumber, quartered lengthways and sliced

sea salt and freshly ground black pepper

for the nasi goreng paste

3 tbsp groundnut oil

4 large garlic cloves, roughly chopped

2 large shallots, roughly chopped

15g (½ oz) roasted unsalted peanuts

3 red chillies, seeded and roughly chopped

2.5cm (1in) piece fresh root ginger, peeled and roughly chopped

1 tbsp tomato purée

1 tbsp Thai fish sauce

1 tbsp ketap manis

Pan-fried Scallops with Chorizo, Apples and Mashed Potatoes

Scallops and mash are a great pairing and make for fantastic comfort food. Now, mix in a bit of chorizo, with its incredible orange oil, and some apple, and you have comfort and gastro in the same bite.

Serves 4

for the scallops

3 tbsp olive oil

16 scallops, with or without roes

1 tbsp butter

2 Cox's or Braeburn apples, cut into small cubes

3 fresh chorizo sausages, cut into small cubes

for the mash

6 largish potatoes, peeled (I love Maris Pipers for mash)

50g (2oz) butter

50ml (2fl oz) milk or cream

sea salt and freshly ground black pepper

Step one Place the potatoes in a large pan, cover with cold water and add 1 teaspoon sea salt. Bring to the boil, and cook for 15 minutes or until softened and cooked through. Drain well and tip into a bowl. Pop the potatoes, one at a time, into the potato ricer and squeeze them back into the pan: lots of squiggles of potato will spill out and there will be no lumps! (If you only have a classic potato masher, simply return the potatoes to the pan they were cooked in and mash like crazy until the potatoes are smooth.) Place the pan on the hob over a medium heat and push the potato up the sides of the pan so you can see the base. Melt the butter and milk or cream in the centre of the base, then whip together with the fluffy potato until it holds its shape but isn't too stiff. Season with plenty of salt and pepper.

Step two Heat 1 tablespoon of oil in a pan until it starts to shimmer. Lay the scallops in a circle round the pan. Add the butter and let it foam up. Cook the scallops for about 1 minute on each side, or until crisp and golden. Divide the hot mashed potato between 4 bowls. Remove the scallops from the pan and pop 4 into each bowl of mash.

Step three To the same pan, add the remaining 2 tablespoons of oil, the apples and chorizo and stir-fry over a high heat for 2–3 minutes or until golden. Divide the chorizo and apples between the bowls of scallops and mash, and pour over the oil from the pan before serving.

This recipe is also delicious if you use black pudding instead of chorizo.

Crispy-skin Salmon with Wasabi Soba Noodles

This is an interpretation of one of my best friend Abbey's dishes, and I love it! It holds fond memories of me, Abbey and Julie munching away at it over a glass of wine while having a good old girly catch-up. It is a really tasty dish that you can throw together very quickly: the heady wasabi and creamy mayonnaise make a terrific dressing for the aromatic and bitey soba noodles, and the crunchy veggies add texture. Abbey and I had a catering company for a few years and we used to serve this dish on Chinese soup spoons as canapés.

Step one Cook the noodles according to the packet instructions. Meanwhile, mix the soy sauce, mirin, grated ginger and sugar in a bowl. Soak the salmon steaks in this marinade for 5 minutes, or longer if you like, although it's not really necessary.

Step two To make the noodle sauce, mix together the mayonnaise and wasabi in a mixing bowl. Add the cooked warm noodles, along with all the vegetables, and mix thoroughly. Divide between 4 plates.

Step three Heat the oil in a frying pan. Remove the salmon from the marinade and wipe off any excess. Reserve the rest of the marinade. Fry the salmon, skin-side down, for 6 minutes or until the skin has turned really golden and crisp, being careful not to cook it too quickly or the sugar in the marinade will burn. Turn the salmon over and cook on the other side for a couple of minutes or until golden. Remove the salmon from the pan with a fish slice and drain on kitchen paper.

Step four Pour away the oil, then add the reserved marinade and leave it to bubble away until slightly syrupy. Lay a piece of salmon on each plate, drizzle with a little of the marinade and sprinkle over some sesame seeds.

Serves 4

250g (9oz) soba noodles (black ones will look beautiful)

6 tbsp soy sauce

4 tbsp mirin (sweet rice wine)

2.5cm (1in) piece of fresh root ginger, peeled and grated

1 tsp sugar

4 salmon steaks, skin on

4 tbsp mayonnaise

1 tsp wasabi

50g (2oz) sugar-snap peas, sliced on the diagonal

½ red pepper, seeded and cut into matchsticks

1 medium carrot, cut into matchsticks

1 spring onion, cut into matchsticks

3 tbsp groundnut oil

1 tbsp sesame seeds

Blackened Snapper with Sweet Potato Mash and Coconut Sauce

I first got the recipe for this coconut sauce, when I used to work in Camden from the famous Caribbean restaurant, the Mango Room.

Serves 2

for the fish

½ tsp ground cumin

½ tsp chilli powder

½ tsp celery salt

½ tsp coriander

½ tsp paprika

4 x 150g (5oz) thick fillets of red snapper

a squeeze of lemon

for the mash

4 sweet potatoes

2 tbsp butter

2 spring onions, sliced

salt and freshly ground black pepper

for the coconut sauce

3 tbsp olive oil

1 onion, chopped

1 tbsp curry powder

3 garlic cloves, finely chopped

2 tsp paprika

3 tomatoes, chopped

400ml (¾ pint) coconut milk

1 tsp thyme leaves

2 spring onions, cut into matchsticks

1 red chilli, chopped

½ tsp sugar

a squeeze of lime

Step one Put the sweet potatoes for the mash into the oven and bake for 45 minutes until softened all the way through. Scoop out the flesh from the skins and beat together with the butter, salt and pepper and spring onions until totally mashed.

Step two Heat the oil for the sauce in a sauté pan over a medium heat. Add the onions and let them cook for 5 minutes until they are transparent. Add the curry powder, garlic and paprika. Cook the spices for 1–2 minutes stirring constantly and then add the tomatoes, coconut milk and thyme. Cook gently for 10 minutes or until the tomatoes have broken down and all the flavours have infused. Strain the sauce rejecting what's left in the strainer and keeping the liquid, then season with salt, pepper, sugar and lime.

Step three For the fish, mix the spices and dust the fish fillets evenly with the spice mix. Heat a pan on high and pan-fry the fish, skin-side down for 4 minutes turning and finishing it off on the other side for about 2 minutes. Squeeze a lemon over the fish before serving. Place a few dollops of mash on each plate and top with fish. Form a moat with the sauce and garnish with the chilli and spring onions to serve.

Lemon Sole Goujons with Mushy Peas and Sweet Potato Wedges

These yummy goujons with sweet potato wedges are a great twist on traditional British fish and chips.

Step one Preheat the oven to 200°C/400°F/gas 6. Place the sweet potato wedges into a large roasting tin, then drizzle over the oil, turning them to coat them all over. Roast in the oven for 25–30 minutes, turning halfway through cooking, until the sweet potato wedges are crisp and golden brown and cooked through.

Step two Meanwhile, for the lemon sole goujons, sprinkle the flour onto a plate. Beat the eggs in a bowl. Mix together the breadcrumbs, cayenne pepper and lemon zest until well combined, then sprinkle the mixture onto a separate plate. Season the fish pieces, to taste, with salt and freshly ground black pepper. Dredge each piece of fish first in the flour, then dip it into the beaten egg, then roll it in the breadcrumbs until completely coated.

Step three Heat the oil in a frying pan over a medium heat until a breadcrumb sizzles and turns golden brown when dipped into it. Add the coated fish pieces to the pan, in batches, and fry for 2–3 minutes each side until crisp, golden and cooked through. Remove the fried fish pieces from the pan using a slotted spoon and set aside to drain on kitchen paper. Repeat the process with the remaining fish pieces.

Step four Meanwhile, for the mushy peas, cook the peas in a pan of boiling, salted water for 3–4 minutes, or until just tender. Drain well and crush using a fork or potato masher. Stir the crème fraîche and mint sauce (or fresh mint) into the crushed peas and season, to taste, with salt and freshly ground black pepper. Place in a small bowl and serve along side the goujons and sweet potato wedges.

Serves 4

for the sweet potato wedges

2 sweet potatoes, skin on, cut into wedges

2 tbsp olive oil

for the lemon sole goujons

50g (2oz) plain flour

2 free-range eggs

100g (4oz) fresh breadcrumbs

½ tsp cayenne pepper

½ lemon, zest only

4 fillets lemon sole, skin removed, cut into 1cm (½ inch) strips

4 tbsp olive oil

salt and freshly ground black pepper

for the mushy peas

200g (7oz) peas

1 tbsp crème fraîche

½ tsp ready-made mint sauce

salt and freshly ground black pepper

for the lemon mayonnaise

squeeze lemon juice, to taste

3 tbsp ready-made mayonnaise

Smoked Haddock and Crevette Fishcakes with a Poached Egg

Paired with smoked fish and a soft poached egg, this has to be one of the most comforting meals anyone could ask for.

Serves 4

200g (7oz) potatoes, peeled and cubed

400g (14oz) undyed smoked haddock fillet

20 crevettes (cooked, shell-on prawns), shelled, or 200g (7oz) small shelled cooked prawns

2 tbsp chopped mixed herbs, such as chervil, dill and parsley

grated zest of 1 lemon

100g (4oz) plain flour

1 egg, lightly beaten

200g (7oz) breadcrumbs

olive oil

sea salt and freshly ground black pepper

4 eggs

steamed spinach, to serve

Step one To make the fishcakes, put the potato cubes into a small pan, cover with cold water and add a pinch of salt. Bring to the boil and cook for 10–15 minutes, or until soft, then drain. Pop the potato cubes back into the pan and mash them, without adding any butter or milk. Transfer the mashed potatoes to a bowl and leave to cool.

Step two Lay the haddock skin-side up in a frying pan and cover with cold water. Bring to the boil and boil for 1 minute, then switch off the heat. Leave the fish to cool for 10 minutes in the pan of water. This will produce a perfectly poached piece of fish.

Step three Remove the fish from the water and leave it to drain on kitchen paper. When the haddock has cooled enough to touch, peel off the skin and break up the flesh up into large flakes. Add the flaked fish to the potatoes, then add the peeled prawns, mixed herbs and lemon zest, and season to taste. Shape into 4 even-sized balls and flatten them.

Step four Put the flour, beaten egg and breadcrumbs on three separate plates. Dip the fishcakes first into the flour, then into the beaten egg, then into the breadcrumbs. In a frying pan, heat a good lug of olive oil until the oil sizzles when you pop in a few breadcrumbs. Lay the fishcakes in the pan and fry over a medium heat for 3–4 minutes on each side. Remove the fishcakes from the pan and drain on kitchen paper. Keep them warm in the oven while you poach the eggs.

Step five Bring a medium-sized pan of water to the boil and poach the eggs, one at a time. Reheat them before serving. Serve each fishcake on a bed of spinach, topped with an egg.

Smoked Salmon, Goats' Cheese and Pea Tart

A fantastic dish for a family summer lunch.

Step one Preheat the oven to 200°C/400°F/gas 6. Dust a work surface and the rolling pin with flour and roll out the pastry to the thickness of a 50-pence piece. Fold one end of the pastry over the rolling pin and quickly transfer it to a 22cm/8¾in loose-based tart tin. Chill in the fridge or freezer for 20 minutes.

Step two To bake blind, line the raw pastry case with a sheet of greaseproof paper. Fill with ceramic baking beans and bake in the oven for 20 minutes, then remove the beans and greaseproof lining and bake for another 10 minutes until the pastry is golden. Leave it to cool in the case for 20 minutes, then carefully trim the edges of the pastry with a knife.

Step three Reduce the oven temperature to 170°C/340°F/gas 4. Heat the olive oil in a small frying pan. Add the red onion and fry on a fairly high heat for 5 minutes, or until slightly charred but beginning to soften. Remove from the pan and set aside.

Step four Pour the white wine into a pan and boil on a high heat for 5 minutes, or until the wine has reduced by two-thirds and is syrupy. Pour into a mixing bowl and leave to cool for 5 minutes. Meanwhile, neatly scatter the red onions, smoked salmon strips, peas and goats' cheese into the pastry tart case.

Step five Add the eggs, cream and Parmesan to the bowl containing the reduced wine, and whisk together. Season well with salt and pepper, and stir in the herbs. Pour into a measuring jug.

Step six Place the tart case on a baking sheet and pour in the liquid – the mixture will come fairly high up the edge of the tart case. Bake on the bottom shelf of the oven for 30 minutes, or until the tart begins to turn golden. You want it still to have a little wobble, but it should not be runny at all. Remove from the oven and leave to cool on a wire rack. Serve warm or cold.

Serves 6

for the pastry

1 x 500g packet all-butter shortcrust pastry

a pinch of salt

120g (4½ oz) ice-cold butter, cubed

1 free-range egg, whisked

flour for dusting

for the filling

2 tsp olive oil

1 small red onion, cut into small wedges

100ml (3⅛ fl oz) white wine

120g (4½ oz) smoked salmon, cut into thin strips

120g (4½ oz) fresh peas

100g (4oz) soft goat's cheese

3 free-range eggs

150ml (¼ pint) double cream

30g (1¼ oz) Parmesan, grated

1 tbsp chopped mixed fresh herbs, such as dill, mint and chives

sea salt and freshly ground black pepper

Griddled Indian Salmon with Spiced Lentil Salad

A spice rub can transform plain chicken or fish into a masterpiece.

Serves 4

for the spice rub

1 tsp ground cumin

1 tsp ground coriander

½ tsp turmeric

¼ tsp cayenne pepper

½ tsp sea salt

1 garlic clove, grated

1½ tbsp vegetable oil

4 fresh salmon fillets

for the salad

200g (7oz) Puy lentils

3cm (1⅛ in) piece of fresh ginger, peeled and sliced

1 tsp turmeric

3 spring onions, sliced

1 red pepper, seeded and chopped

¼ cucumber, cut into small pieces

a small bunch fresh coriander leaves

for the dressing

1 tsp ground cumin

1 tsp ground coriander

¼ tsp cayenne pepper

½ heaped tsp sea salt

1 garlic clove, grated

juice of ½ lemon

2–3 tbsp extra virgin olive oil

Step one To make the spice rub, mix all the dry spices together in a bowl. Add the garlic and oil. Mix thoroughly and rub over the salmon fillets. Chill in the fridge for at least 1 hour.

Step two Place the lentils, sliced ginger and turmeric in a large saucepan. Cover with water and bring to the boil. Reduce the heat and simmer for approximately 20 minutes until the lentils are tender. (You may need to add more water as the lentils absorb quite a lot while cooking.) Strain off any excess water and leave to cool.

Step three Heat a griddle pan on high and when it starts to smoke lay on the salmon fillets. Grill for 3 minutes on each side or until you are confident the salmon has just cooked through. You really want it a little underdone so it's juicy and opaque in the middle, but feel free to cook it however you like.

Step four In the meantime, make the dressing. Put all the ingredients in a small bowl and mix thoroughly. When the lentils have cooled, add the spring onions, red pepper, cucumber and coriander leaves, mix gently and then add the dressing and mix gently once more. Spoon the lentil salad onto plates and top with the fillets of salmon. Drizzle any of the salmon juices over and get stuck in!

Bright Green Pea and Goats' Cheese Risotto

This risotto is bright green as it has puréed peas running through it.
I would always use frozen peas as they are so much sweeter and really
add depth to the dish. The truffle oil is optional, but it's a great store-
cupboard ingredient and makes a really sexy addition to loads of dishes.

Step one Cook the peas in some water with the mint. When cooked, drain 400g (14oz) of the peas, saving the rest for garnish, and blitz in a blender with the mint to a smooth green purée. Keep the peas warm.

Step two Heat the oil in a large, heavy-based saucepan over a low heat. Add the leeks and sauté about 5 minutes. Add the rice and toast in the hot oil for 1 minute. Add the wine and stir until absorbed. Add one ladleful of the hot stock, adjust the heat to maintain a gentle simmer, and cook, stirring continuously, until the liquid is absorbed. Continue adding the stock, one ladleful at a time and stirring continuously, until the rice is just tender but slightly firm in the center and the mixture is creamy – this takes about 20 minutes.

Step three Now add the mushy peas, whole peas, truffle oil, Parmesan, butter and crème fraîche and stir in quickly. Taste and season if needed. Add the lemon zest and juice. Stir in the goats' cheese until it is molten and melting throughout the risotto. Top with the pea shoots, more Parmesan and truffle oil, and serve.

Serves 4

600g (1¼ lb) frozen peas

a small bunch fresh mint

1 tbsp olive oil

2 leeks, finely chopped

400g (14oz) arborio rice

1 glass white wine

600ml (1 pint) chicken or vegetable stock, hot

1 tsp white truffle oil, plus more for serving

freshly grated Parmesan cheese

a knob of butter

2 tbsp crème fraîche

grated zest and juice of a lemon

1 log goats' cheese

1 punnet of pea shoots

salt and freshly ground black pepper

Veggie Moussaka

A stonkingly good dish to feed a pack if you have a veggie guest coming over. To save time, you can use a jar of ready-made fresh cheese sauce.

Serves 6

3 tbsp olive oil

1 large courgette, chopped

1 onion, finely chopped

1 red pepper, seeded and finely chopped

1 yellow pepper, seeded and finely chopped

3–4 garlic cloves

1 tsp cinnamon

2 tbsp tomato purée

2 x 400g (14oz) tins chopped tomatoes

1 x 400g (14oz) tin green lentils, or 200g (7oz) dried lentils cooked in boiling water until tender

a small bunch of fresh parsley, chopped

3 aubergines, sliced

sea salt and freshly ground black pepper

for the white sauce

30g (1¼ oz) butter

30g (1¼ oz) plain flour

500ml (17fl oz) milk

1 ball mozzarella, chopped

a good grating of nutmeg

sea salt and freshly ground black pepper

Step one Preheat the oven to 180°C/350°F/gas 4. Heat 1 tablespoon of the olive oil in a pan and fry the courgettes until golden. Remove from the pan with a slotted spoon then add another tablespoon of olive oil to the pan along with the onions and peppers. Cook for 15 minutes until softened, super sweet and reduced in volume.

Step two Add the garlic and cook for a further minute, then add the cinnamon, tomato purée and chopped tomatoes. Simmer for 10 minutes then stir in the lentils and cook for a further 20 minutes. Stir in the parsley, then leave to cool a little.

Step three Meanwhile brush the aubergines with the remaining olive oil and season. Griddle or fry on both sides until cooked through and completely soft and tender. In a roughly 20 x 30cm (8 x 12in) ovenproof lasagne dish, layer up the aubergine slices and lentil mix.

Step four To make the sauce, melt the butter in a pan. Stir in the flour and cook for 1 minute. Remove from the heat and gradually whisk in the milk, little by little, stirring like crazy until combined and smooth. Add the mozzarella and nutmeg and season to taste. Spoon over the aubergine and lentil dish to cover completely. Bake for 45–50 minutes until the top is golden. Serve with a green salad.

Injera with Sweet Potato and Red Lentil Stew and Cauliflower, Beetroot and Carrot Salad

Injera is an Ethopian pancake. It is great to fill with stews and currys.

Step one Mix all of the dry ingredients for the injera together well. Stir in the fizzy water and mix to a smooth batter that should have the thin consistency of pancake batter. Heat a large cast-iron skillet over a medium–low flame and wipe with kitchen paper soaked in a little oil. Pour about half a cup of the batter at a time into the skillet and spread with a spatula to make as large a crêpe as possible. It should be thicker than a conventional crêpe but thin enough to fold. Bake it in the skillet until all the bubbles on the top burst and begin to dry out, this should take about 2–3 minutes. Carefully turn the injera and cook on the second side for another minute or two. Remove the injera to a warm platter and repeat with the rest of the batter, wiping the skillet clean with the kitchen paper towel each time. Sprinkle each pancake with a little lemon juice.

Step two Pop the onion, garlic, and ginger for the stew into a food processor or blender and blitz until smooth. Heat the oil in a large, heavy-bottomed saucepan and add the turmeric, paprika and cayenne pepper, and stir rapidly to colour the oil and cook the spices through. This should take about 30 seconds. Add the onion purée and sauté for around 5 minutes on a medium heat until it starts to go golden, then add the lentils and the stock. Bring to a boil and simmer for about 30–40 minutes until the lentils are cooked through and fall apart. Add water if necessary to keep the stew from drying out. Stir in salt and pepper to taste.

Step three Mix the salad ingredients together and leave to macerate for 30 minutes. Serve the injera hot and stuffed with a couple of tablespoons of the stew and some salad, then finish with finely chopped spring onions.

Serves 6

for the injera

100g (4oz) whole wheat flour
200g (7oz) plain flour
1 tsp baking powder
½ tsp sea salt
300ml (½ pint) fizzy water
2 lemons, juiced

for the lentil stew

1 onion, chopped
2 garlic cloves, chopped
3cm (1¼in) ginger, grated
2 tbsp vegetable oil
1 tsp ground turmeric
2 tsp paprika
1 tsp cayenne pepper
250g (9oz) red lentils
250g (9oz) sweet potatoes, peeled and chopped
600ml (1 pint) vegetable stock
sea salt and freshly ground black pepper

for the salad

½ small head cauliflower, cut into small florets
1 large carrot, grated
1 raw beetroot, grated
pinch of salt
2 tbsp extra virgin olive oil
3 tbsp lemon juice
1 tsp sugar
¼ tsp red-pepper flakes
2 spring onions, finely chopped

Keralan egg curry

A quick, simple dish that's delicious garnished with coriander leaves, and served with chapattis or rice.

Serves 4

4 large free-range eggs, hard-boiled

2–3 tbsp vegetable oil

1 onion, finely chopped

3–4 garlic cloves, finely chopped

3cm (1¼ in) piece fresh ginger root, peeled and grated

1–2 green chillies, seeded and finely chopped

½ tbsp tomato purée

¼ tsp sea salt

¾ tsp ground turmeric

½ tsp ground cumin

½ tsp ground coriander

¾ tsp garam masala

1 tomato, finely chopped

200ml (7fl oz) coconut milk

100g (4oz) petite pois

2 tbsp coriander leaves, chopped

chapattis or rice, to serve

Step one Remove and discard the shell from the hard-boiled eggs, halve and set aside. Blend the oil, onion, garlic, ginger, green chillies, tomato purée, salt and spices together. Heat a wok and add the paste and fry for 3–4 minutes.

Step two Add the tomato, coconut milk and peas and simmer for 5 minutes. For the last 2 minutes of cooking add the boiled eggs. Serve the egg curry hot, garnished with coriander leaves, with chapattis or rice.

Muttar Paneer

I cannot even remember the first time I had muttar paneer, but what I can tell you is that it has to be one of the most delicious dishes, veggie or not. The paneer cheese has a texture like tofu, although it is more often compared to cottage cheese. The peas burst with each mouthful, and the mild curry base is so flexible you can use it with whatever you like.

Step one Whizz together all the curry paste ingredients in a blender.

Step two Heat a wok or pan, then add the vegetable oil for the paneer, a tablespoon at a time. When it's hot, fry the paneer until golden brown. Scoop it out with a slotted spoon and set aside to drain on some kitchen paper.

Step three Add the paste and fry for about 5 minutes, or until it starts to brown a little and the room fills with a spicy aroma. Add the tomatoes and stock and simmer for 10 minutes until thickened. Add the paneer and the peas and cook for 5 minutes. Season to taste and serve with naan bread.

Swap the peas for a bag of baby spinach and you've got a great saag paneer!

Serves 4

2 tbsp vegetable oil

250g (9oz) paneer (Indian cheese, found in the cheese section of the supermarket), cut into chunks

4 very ripe tomatoes, roughly chopped

300ml (½ pint) vegetable stock

300g (11oz) frozen peas

naan bread, to serve

sea salt and freshly ground black pepper

for the curry paste

2 tbsp vegetable oil

1 onion, chopped

2.5cm (1in) piece of fresh root ginger, peeled and chopped

4 garlic cloves, chopped

a pinch of garam masala

2 tsp ground turmeric

½ tsp cayenne pepper

Roasted Aubergine, Mint and Yoghurt Salad

This dish came about by accident! We were filming on location and had loads of barbecued aubergine, so I wanted to make something with it. After a rummage in the fridge I came up with this recipe, and it's addictive. Stuff it into pitta bread or serve it with roast lamb – either way, it's pretty fantastic.

Serves 4

2 aubergines, halved lengthways

1 garlic bulb

8 tbsp extra virgin olive oil

juice of ½ lemon

250g (9oz) Greek yoghurt

a small bunch fresh coriander, stems discarded, leaves chopped

a small bunch fresh mint, stems discarded, leaves chopped

sea salt and freshly ground black pepper

Step one Preheat the oven to 200°C/400°F/gas 6. Lay the aubergines, cut-side up, and the garlic bulb on a baking tray, and brush them with 4 tablespoons of olive oil. Season with salt and pepper. Bake for 30 minutes, or until the aubergines start to char and the garlic is soft. Leave to cool for 15 minutes.

Step two Carefully cut the garlic bulb in half and squeeze the soft flesh onto a chopping board. With the back of a knife, squash the garlic until it forms a paste. Place the aubergines on the same chopping board, remove and discard the stalks, then chop the flesh into small chunks until it resembles a chopped salad. Drizzle with a good 2 tablespoons of olive oil and add the lemon juice.

Step three Spread the yoghurt on a serving plate and top with the aubergine salad. Scatter over the fresh herbs and drizzle with a good lug of olive oil before serving.

my KITCHEN TABLE For a video masterclass on knife skills, go to www.mykitchentable.co.uk/videos/knifeskills

Pan-Fried Haloumi with Black Bean, Avocado and Chilli Salsa

Traditionally, haloumi cheese is served with Cypriot or Turkish accompaniments, but it works well with any strong flavours. Here I have used classic Mexican ingredients, one of the key components being chipotle chillies, which are smoked, dried jalapeños. They have such a distinct smoky flavour and will be a revelation to chilli fans.

Serves 4

2 x 200g (7oz) packs haloumi cheese, each cut into 10 slices

1 tbsp olive oil

for the salsa

200g (7oz) tinned black-eyed beans, drained and rinsed

1 large ripe but firm avocado, peeled and chopped

1 large vine tomato, seeded and chopped

2 spring onions, chopped

1 chipotle chilli, soaked overnight in boiling water, then drained and chopped

1 garlic clove, grated

½ tsp ground cumin

juice of 1 lime

1 tbsp extra virgin olive oil

sea salt and freshly ground black pepper

Step one Brush the haloumi slices with olive oil and lay them in a hot pan on a medium heat. Pan-fry for 2 minutes on each side, until golden brown, then remove to a large serving platter.

Step two In a mixing bowl, combine all the salsa ingredients. Adjust the seasoning to taste, and spoon the salsa over the haloumi. Serve immediately.

If you can't find chipotle chillies you may be able to find chipotle chilli Tabasco in your local supermarket. Failing that, soaking a nice fat, fresh, red chilli overnight will do the job.

Caramelised Fennel and Stilton Tart

The aniseed notes of fennel work magic when paired with Stilton cheese, and what better way to show them off than in an aromatic tart. You can make them individual for a dinner party starter too.

Makes 6 slices

plain flour, for dusting

1 x 500g packet all-butter shortcrust pastry

a good knob of butter

3 fennel bulbs, trimmed, halved and finely sliced

1 tbsp of Pernod, if you have it to hand

1 tsp brown sugar

3 egg yolks

150ml (¼ pint) double cream

150g (5oz) Stilton cheese, crumbled

sea salt and freshly ground black pepper

Step one Preheat the oven to 200°C/400°F/gas 6. Roll out the pastry on a lightly floured surface, then line a 25cm (10in) tart case. Chill in the fridge or freezer for 20 minutes.

Step two Line the case with baking paper and fill with baking beans. Bake blind for 20 minutes, then remove the beans and and paper, bake for a further 10 minutes until the pastry is golden. Leave to cool in the case.

Step three While the pastry is cooling, melt the butter in a pan and cook the fennel over a lowish heat for 10 minutes, stirring occasionally. Add the Pernod, if using, and the sugar and cook for a further 10 minutes until sticky and golden. You must make sure all the liquid has been evaporated. Remove from the heat and let them cool a little.

Step four Meanwhile, gently beat together the egg yolks and cream. Add in the Stilton and season with salt and pepper. Fill the cooled tart case with a layer of fennel, then cover with the Stilton filling and bake for 20–25 minutes until just set and golden. Leave to cool a bit before serving. I'd say it is at its best served warm.

Potato, Onion and Taleggio Pies

The classic combination of potato, onion and cheese is – as ever – a winner, but the addition of oozy Taleggio, makes it all the sexier!

Step one To make the suet pastry, sift the flour into a large mixing bowl and add a pinch of salt. Add some freshly milled black pepper, then add the suet and mix it into the flour using the blade of a knife.

Step two When it's evenly blended, add a few drops of cold water and start to mix with the knife, using curving movements and turning the mixture around until it begins to get really claggy and sticky.

Step three Now go in with your hands and bring it all together until you have a nice, smooth elastic dough, which leaves the bowl clean. It's worth noting that suet pastry always needs more water than other types, so if it is still a bit dry just go on adding a few drops at a time.

Step four Heat the olive oil in a smallish pan, then fry the onions on a low heat for 20 minutes or until soft, sweet and golden. Set aside to cool for 10 minutes, then mix with the potato slices, Taleggio cheese and some salt and pepper.

Step five Preheat oven to 180°C/350°F/gas 4. On a floured surface, roll out the pastry to the thickness of a £1 coin. Cut out 8 squares measuring about 13 x 13cm (5 x 5in). Divide the potato and cheese filling between each of the squares, making sure you place the filling right in the centre, and then brush the edges with the beaten egg. Bring all four corners together over the filling, pinching the edges together to make a sealed purse. Transfer to a baking tray and brush each pie generously with egg. Chill in the fridge for 15 minutes.

Step six Bake for 30 minutes until golden and the cheese has melted. Best served warm with a crispy green salad.

Serves 4

for the pastry

350g self-raising flour, plus extra for dusting

200g (7oz) vegetable suet

7–10 tbsp ice-cold water

sea salt and freshly ground black pepper

for the filling

1 tbsp olive oil

2 onions, thinly sliced

1 large baking potato, peeled and thinly sliced

100g (4oz) Tellagio cheese, sliced into small cubes

1 portion of wholemeal suet pastry

1 egg, beaten

sea salt and freshly ground black pepper

Dead Posh Cheese and Truffle Soufflé for Two

This may sound like some mega-gastro experience, but I promise you'll find soufflé-making much less intimidating than it's made out to be.

Serves 2

15g (½ oz) butter, plus extra for greasing the dish

30g (1oz) Parmesan cheese, plus extra for dusting

1 tbsp plain flour

150ml (¼ pint) milk

50g (2oz) truffle pecorino cheese

3 eggs, separated

1 tsp truffle oil (optional)

sea salt and freshly ground black pepper

Step one Preheat the oven to 200°C/400°F/gas 6. Grease a medium-sized ramekin (big enough for 2 servings) with butter, then grate a fine layer of Parmesan over it to coat the inside of the dish.

Step two Melt the butter in a small pan, stir in the flour and cook over a low heat for 1 minute. Remove from the heat and gradually add the milk, whisking as you go to avoid any lumps forming. When the milk has been combined, return to the heat and keep stirring with a wooden spoon while it simmers lightly. Scrape the bottom of the pan – milk burns easily. After about 2 minutes, when the sauce has thickened, remove the pan from the heat. Stir in the truffle cheese, then the Parmesan, egg yolks and truffle oil, if using, and season well. Leave the mixture to cool for 10 minutes.

Step three In a clean, dry mixing bowl, whisk the egg whites until they are stiff, but not too solid. Mix a spoonful of egg white into the cheese sauce, to loosen it. Now pour the cheese mixture into the rest of the egg white and, using a metal spoon, fold them together as quickly and lightly as possible – try not to knock the air out of the soufflé mixture as this will affect the rise and texture of the dish.

Step four Pour the mixture into the ramekin and level off the top. Push the tip of a knife 0.5cm (¼in) into the edge of the ramekin and slide it right round, as if you're pulling the soufflé mixture away from the edge – this is what will make it rise. Put the soufflé on a baking sheet and place in the oven to cook for 18 minutes, until it's risen, firm but not too stiff – it should still be gooey in the middle. Remove from the oven and serve straight away. It will sink a little bit after a few minutes, so the sooner you serve it, the better the 'wow' factor!

Sticky Banoffee Pudding

This is my boyfriend Dean's recipe. While he is a fantastic cook, he is so lazy he never cooks for me, except for this. And my God, does it make up for it! The banana is terrific with the toffeeish dates and keeps the pudding really moist. Remove the bananas and you've got a classic sticky toffee pudding.

Step one Preheat the oven to 180°C/350°F/gas 4 and butter a 23cm (9in) baking dish. Place the dates in a small pan and cover with the hot tea. Bring to the boil and cook for 3–4 minutes, until the dates have softened, then stir in the bicarbonate of soda.

Step two Cream together the butter and sugar until light and fluffy, then add the beaten eggs gradually. Fold in the flour, bananas, mixed spice and the date mixture, then pour into the baking dish. Bake for 30–35 minutes, until the top is springy and a skewer comes out clean when inserted into the centre.

Step three While the pudding is cooking, make the sauce. Put the muscovado sugar, butter and cream into a pan, place over a low heat and melt until the sugar has dissolved. Increase the heat and simmer for 3–4 minutes, or until the sauce is a light toffee colour. Serve the pudding with the warm sauce and a big scoop of vanilla ice cream or clotted cream.

Serves 6

250g (9oz) dates, stoned and chopped

250ml (7fl oz) hot black tea, made with 1 teabag

1 tsp bicarbonate of soda

85g (3½ oz) unsalted butter, softened, plus extra for greasing

175g (6oz) caster sugar

2 large eggs, beaten

175g (6oz) self-raising flour, sieved

3 bananas, roughly mashed

1 tsp ground mixed spice

vanilla ice cream, or clotted cream, to serve

for the sauce

100g (4oz) light muscovado sugar

100g (4oz) unsalted butter

150ml (¼ pint) double cream

Baileys Chocolate Croissant Butter Pudding

I came across a similar recipe to this while working at BBC Good Food. It was a pivotal point in my pudding-making career, as I had never before tasted anything quite so amazing. I have made it my own (and even better) by adding even more booze to the custard and simply making it really gooey. Be warned: it is one of those puddings that has you believing that you can eat the whole lot.

Serves 6

50g (2oz) golden caster sugar

1 large egg, plus 5 yolks

300ml (½ pint) Baileys Irish Cream liqueur

400ml (14fl oz) double cream

butter, for greasing

6–8 chocolate croissants, torn into pieces

75g (3oz) light muscovado sugar

for the butterscotch sauce

100g (4oz) light muscovado sugar

100g (4oz) butter

150ml (¼ pint) double cream

Step one Preheat the oven to 200°C/400°F/gas 6. In a bowl, whisk together the caster sugar, whole egg and egg yolks. Put the Baileys and double cream into a pan and bring to the boil. Whisk this into the egg mixture, then leave to cool slightly into a custard.

Step two Lightly grease a 30 x 20cm (12 x 8in) baking dish with butter. Place a layer of croissant pieces in the base and add a generous sprinkle of muscovado sugar and a little of the egg custard. Keep on layering croissants, sugar and custard in the same way, finishing off with a sprinkling of sugar. Let the pudding sit for 10 minutes so it soaks up all the custard.

Step three Bake for 18–20 minutes, until the pudding is puffed up, golden and crisp (the muscovado sugar will give a tasty and sticky finish). Meanwhile, make the sauce. Place the sugar and butter in a pan and stir over a medium heat until the sugar has dissolved. Pour in the cream and bring to the boil. Reduce the heat and simmer for 3–4 minutes, until dark and sticky. To serve, scoop out servings of the pudding and pour over a little of the warm sauce.

Raspberry and Almond Roly-Poly

Frangipane and raspberries add a different dimension to a familiar pud.

Step one To make the pastry, sift the flour and the sugar into a large mixing bowl and add a pinch of salt. Add the orange zest, then add the suet, mixing it in with the blade of a knife. When it's evenly blended, add a few drops of cold milk and start to mix with the knife, turning the mixture around until it gets really sticky. Now go in with your hands and bring it all together until you have a nice, smooth elastic dough.

Step two To make the filling, warm the raspberries in a pan with a tablespoon of icing sugar until the fruits begin to soften. Increase the heat, so the juices boil and become jammy. Pour into a bowl, then stir in the raspberry jam. Leave to cool.

Step three Mix together the almonds, butter, egg, amaretto and remaining icing sugar to form a smooth paste. Butter and lightly flour a large sheet of greaseproof paper (40 x 30cm/16 x 12 in) and sit it on a bigger sheet of foil. Put a steamer onto simmer.

Step four On a lightly floured surface, roll the pastry dough into a rectangle about 22 x 25cm/8¾ x 10in. Firstly, spread with a thin layer of the almond paste so that it covers the whole sheet of pastry, next spread the cooled raspberry mixture on top of the almond paste, leaving a 2cm/¾in border around the edge.

Step five Moisten the border with cold water or milk before rolling into a cylinder. Tuck the ends under to avoid the jam pouring out. With the long join underneath, lay the roly-poly in the centre of the greaseproof paper. Fold over the paper and foil edges, leaving enough space above the pudding to allow it to rise. Squeeze the paper ends together tightly to seal them.

Step six Lay the parcel in the steamer, then cover and steam for 1¼–1½ hours, until firm to the touch. Rest for a minute before unwrapping and serving with custard.

Serves 6

for the suet pastry

350g (12oz) self-raising flour, plus extra for dusting

85g (3½ oz) sugar

200g (7oz) beef suet

7–10 tbsp cold milk

zest of 1 orange

pinch of salt

for the filling

175g (6oz) fresh raspberries

50g (2oz) icing sugar plus 1 tbsp

2 tbsp raspberry jam

120g (4½ oz) ground almonds

100g (4oz) unsalted butter, at room temperature

1 free-range egg

1 tbsp amaretto liqueur (optional)

butter and flour, for lining

custard to serve

Lemon and Passion Fruit Self-saucing Pudding

My mum makes the most amazing pudding called lemon surprise tart, which is a crisp pastry tart with gooey lemon sponge in the centre. It is so calorific, though, that I wanted to see if I could make it a little kinder on the waistline. By ditching the crust, you end up with a self-saucing sponge pudding that leaves a wicked custardy curd at the bottom. With the addition of passion fruit, this makes a really light end to your meal, and it's great for Sunday lunch after a heavy roast.

Serves 4–6

50g (2oz) butter, plus extra for greasing

150g (5oz) caster sugar

juice and zest of 1 lemon

120ml (4fl oz) passion fruit juice (if making it yourself, use about 16 passion fruits)

3 large eggs, separated

50g (2oz) plain flour, sifted

250ml (8fl oz) milk

cream and fresh raspberries, to serve

Step one Preheat the oven to 160°C/325°F/gas 3 and grease a baking dish. In a food-processor, whizz together the butter, sugar and lemon zest until pale and creamy. One ingredient at a time, add the lemon juice, passion fruit juice, egg yolks, flour and milk until you have a smooth batter. Whisk the egg whites until firm but not stiff and fold them into the batter.

Step two Pour the batter into the baking dish and place in a baking tray. Half-fill the baking tray with hot water (to make a bain-marie). Put this in the oven and bake for 45–50 minutes, until the top is lightly browned and set and there is a sort of gooey curd below. Remove the dish from the tray and serve hot, with cream and raspberries.

White Chocolate and Honeycomb Cheesecake

This is officially the cheesecake to beat all cheesecakes.

Step one Preheat the oven to 160°C/325°F/gas 3. Line the base of a 23cm (9in) springform cake tin with parchment paper. Stir the biscuit crumbs and sugar together in a bowl. Add the melted butter and stir until evenly mixed. Press the mixture into the base of the tin and bake for 10 minutes. Leave to cool.

Step two Increase the oven temperature to 200°C/400°F/gas 6. To make the filling, put the cream cheese in a food-processor and beat at medium-low speed until creamy, then gradually add the sugar, flour and vanilla extract. One at a time, whisk in the eggs and yolk. Add the soured cream and the melted white chocolate and whisk lightly to blend. The batter should be smooth, light and a little airy. Pour into a mixing bowl and stir in the chopped Crunchie bars.

Step three Brush the insides of the springform tin with melted butter and place it on a baking sheet. Pour in the filling and bake for 15 minutes, then reduce the oven temperature to 110°C/250°F/gas ¼ and bake for a further 25 minutes, or until the filling wobbles slightly when you gently shake the tin. When it has reached this point, turn off the oven and either open the oven door for a cheesecake that's creamy in the centre, or leave it closed if you prefer a drier texture. Either way, leave it to cool in the oven for 2 hours. The cheesecake may crack slightly on top as it cools.

Step four When the cheesecake has cooled, cover loosely with foil and refrigerate for at least 8 hours or overnight. When ready to serve, run a round-bladed knife round the inside of the tin to loosen any stuck edges. Unlock the side of the tin, slide the cheesecake onto a plate, and very carefully slide the parchment paper out from underneath before serving.

Makes 12 slices

200g (7oz) ginger biscuits, whizzed to fine crumbs in a food-processor

1 tbsp golden caster sugar

85ml (3fl oz) butter, melted, plus extra for greasing

for the filling

900g (2lb) full-fat cream cheese

250g (9oz) golden caster sugar

3 tbsp plain flour

1 tsp vanilla extract

3 large eggs, plus 1 egg yolk

300ml (½ pint) soured cream

300g (10½ oz) white chocolate, melted

3 Crunchie bars, trimmed of their chocolate and chopped into pieces

Pineapple Cake with Lime Soured Cream Frosting

I am exposed to all sorts of fantastic foods – I only wish I could describe what it's like walking through Dalston Market in east London on a hot day to the smell of overripe pineapples, the inspiration for this cake, which also evokes memories of exotic holidays. I have taken flavours and influences from the Caribbean – fragrant pineapple, sweet cinnamon, tantalising spices and sour limes – and packed them into this cake, which gives flashes of sunshine in every bite.

Makes 10 slices

200g (7oz) softened butter, plus extra for greasing

200g (7oz) light muscovado sugar

4 large free-range eggs

200g (7oz) self-raising flour

1 tsp baking powder

1 tsp ground cinnamon

1 tsp ground mixed spice

1 x 225g (8 oz) tin crushed pineapple or finely chopped pineapple chunks, with juice

1 tsp vanilla extract

zest and juice of 1 lime

for the lime soured cream frosting

200ml (7fl oz) soured cream

juice and zest of 1 lime, plus extra zest for decoration

100g (4oz) icing sugar

200ml (7fl oz) double cream

Step one Preheat the oven to 170°C/345°F/gas 3. Grease and line a 20cm (8in) springform cake tin. Place the butter and sugar in a mixing bowl and beat together with an electric whisk until pale and fluffy. Add the eggs, one at a time, then sift in the flour, baking powder, cinnamon and mixed spice and stir. Finally stir in the pineapple, vanilla extract and lime zest and juice.

Step two Pour the cake mixture into the tin, leveling off the top as you go, then pop into the oven and bake for 30 minutes. The cake is ready once you can slide a skewer into it and it comes out clean. Remove the cake from the oven and leave to cool in the tin for 15 minutes, then transfer it carefully to a wire rack to cool completely.

Step three To make the frosting, mix together the soured cream, lime zest and juice and icing sugar. Whip the double cream and gently fold into the soured cream mixture. Ice the top of the cake thickly with the icing, decorate with lime zest and serve.

For a video masterclass on icing a cake, go to www.mykitchentable.co.uk/videos/icing

Butter Caramel and Honeycomb Ice Cream

Wickedly decadent, this dessert has a grown-up bittersweet quality to it that little ones don't really appreciate yet adults flock to. But that doesn't mean we have to ignore our childish side: a pack or two of crushed Crunchie bars stirred through the ice cream before it has set in the freezer should do the trick, as the honeycomb in a Crunchie is both sticky and crunchy. Can you imagine? For salted caramel ice cream, instead of Crunchie bars, add three-quarters of a teaspoon of Maldon sea salt halfway through churning.

Serves 6

300g (10½ oz) golden caster sugar

4 tbsp salted butter

500ml (17fl oz) double cream

250ml (8fl oz) whole milk

5 large egg yolks

1 tsp vanilla extract

2 Crunchie bars, chopped, or 2 x 37g (1½ oz) packs of Maltesers, chopped

Step one Put the sugar into a dry frying pan and melt over a low heat until it starts to caramelise – you want it to be a nice mid-brown colour, not too light or too dark. Stir in the butter and half the double cream, then leave to cool a little.

Step two Meanwhile, heat the milk and the remaining cream in a small non-stick pan until bubbles start to rise up the edges. In a separate bowl, whisk together the egg yolks and vanilla extract, then in a slow stream carefully pour in the hot milk, whisking continuously. Pour it back into the pan and, with a wooden spoon, scrape the bottom of the pan while cooking the custard gently on a low heat for a minute or so, until it thickens enough to coat the back of the spoon. (Be really careful – the eggs can scramble quite easily, and if it starts to look grainy it has gone too far.)

Step three Strain the custard into a bowl and leave it to cool, covered with clingfilm. (This will take about 30 minutes, but you can speed the process up by placing the bowl of custard in an ice bath.) Whisk the cold custard into the caramel until combined.

Step four Set up your ice cream machine, pour the caramel custard into it and leave to churn for 20 minutes. Add the chopped Crunchie bars and churn for a further 25 minutes or until smooth and frozen. Transfer the ice cream to a freezerproof container and freeze for at least 2 hours before eating.

Gin and Pink Grapefruit Sorbet

I felt like an old lush even contemplating this recipe, but gin and grapefruit are exceptional together so I gave it a go and as expected, it's a winner! The bitter, sour tang of the grapefruit benefits from the shot of gin, which adds an aromatic cleanness. The taste of it makes me think of sunshine, lawns and croquet, the Queen Mum and all things English. Eat it as a sorbet or as a palate cleanser between courses.

Makes 750ml (1¼ pint)

juice of 7 pink grapefruit

270g (10oz) golden caster sugar

450ml (¾ pint) water

4 tbsp liquid glucose

4 tbsp gin

Step one Put the grapefruit juice, sugar and water into a pan. Heat gently until the sugar dissolves, then stir in the liquid glucose. Bring to the boil and boil for 2–3 minutes. Leave to cool for 30 minutes in an ice bath.

Step two Add the gin to the mixture. Set up your ice-cream machine, pour the liquid into it, and churn the liquid until smooth and frozen. Transfer to a freezer container and freeze for 3–5 hours before eating.

Marbled Chocolate Brownies

The ultimate chocolate fix has got to come from a brownie! There are hundreds of brownie recipes out there, but in this one I have used half plain chocolate and half white, swirling them together to make a gooey, extra-chocolatey treat – a chocoholic's dream!

Step one Heat the oven to 180°C/350°F/gas 4. Grease and line a 23cm (9in) square brownie tin. Break up the chocolate and place the white and plain chocolates into separate heatproof bowls. Cut the butter in half, then cut each half into cubes. Place half the butter with the white chocolate and the other half with the plain. One at a time, pop the bowls into the microwave for 1½ minutes each, stirring halfway through. White chocolate can be a little tricky to work with, so be patient. It may need another 30 seconds.

Step two Add half the sugar and half the eggs to each bowl, then sift half the flour into each of the mixes. Spoon alternate blobs of mixture into the brownie tin to make a patchwork effect. (You can be as messy as you like, but try to remember to layer the white chocolate mixture on top of the brown.) Once all the mixture is in the tin, use a knife to drag it up and down the length of the tin, then repeat in the other direction. This will make beautiful swirly patterns and give it that lovely marbled finish.

Step three Bake for 35 minutes, until firm on top but with a little bit of give. They need to be slightly undercooked to get that moist brownie fudginess.

Step four Leave to cool completely in the tin, then cut the brownies into 16 squares.

Makes 16 squares

200g (7oz) good-quality white chocolate

200g (7oz) plain chocolate, 70% cocoa solids

250g (9oz) butter, plus extra for greasing

300g (10½oz) golden caster sugar

4 eggs, beaten

150g (5oz) plain flour

Earl Grey Chocolate Fudge Cake

Infusing the cake with a hint of Earl Grey tea adds an aromatic tinge.

Makes 10 slices

for the cake

6 Earl Grey teabags

150ml (¼ pint) boiling water

100g (4oz) unsalted butter, plus extra for greasing

125g (4½ oz) plain chocolate, 70% cocoa solids

3 large eggs

150g (5oz) soft dark brown sugar

100g (4oz) light muscovado sugar

250g (9oz) self-raising flour

1 tsp bicarbonate of soda

1 tsp baking powder

3 tbsp Greek yoghurt

for the Earl Grey cream

4 Earl Grey teabags

100ml (4fl oz) boiling water

3 tbsp light muscovado sugar

250g (9oz) cream cheese

for the icing and topping

150g (5oz) plain chocolate, 70% cocoa solids

100ml (4fl oz) double cream

3 tbsp honey

2 tbsp golden caster sugar

1 Earl Grey teabag

Step one Preheat the oven to 180°C/350°F/gas 4. To make the cake, place the teabags in a cup and cover with the boiling water. Leave the tea to stew for 5 minutes, then squeeze out the teabags and discard, leaving the really strong tea to cool a little. Meanwhile, grease and line a 20cm (8in) springform cake tin with butter and a disc of greaseproof paper.

Step two Melt the butter and chocolate in separate bowls and leave to cool, before placing all the cake ingredients, including the tea, into a food-processor. Blend to a smooth batter. Pour the batter into the cake tin and level out the surface. Bake for 50 minutes, or until a metal skewer stuck into the centre comes out clean. Leave to cool in the tin, covered with a clean tea towel, for 2 hours.

Step three To make the Earl Grey cream, place the teabags in a pan and cover with the boiling water. Leave the tea to stew for 5 minutes, then remove the teabags, squeezing out the liquid. Add the sugar to the tea, bring to the boil and boil for 5 minutes or until syrupy. Leave to cool for 10 minutes then whisk into the cream cheese.

Step four Slice the cooled cake in half horizontally. Cover the bottom half with the Earl Grey cream, then place the top of the cake back on. Melt the chocolate for the icing. Add the double cream and honey, then pour the chocolate icing over the cake. Using a spatula, gently tease the icing around the edges until the whole cake is iced.

Step five To make the gold dust, heat the sugar in a small dry frying pan. When it starts to caramelise, empty out the teabag into the caramel and stir the leaves through. Immediately remove from the heat and pour onto a sheet of greaseproof paper. Leave to cool for 10 minutes, then grind up in a pestle and mortar. Sprinkle over the top of the cake and serve.

Blond Rocky Road

Traditional rocky road can sometimes be a bit rich, but using white chocolate mixed with coffee gives a milder biscuit that still has an adult edge. These are super for after-dinner coffee biscuits, and fantastic for a mid-morning pick-me-up.

Step one Heat the double cream in a small, heavy-based pan over a low heat. Add the coffee granules and stir until dissolved, then set aside. In another heavy-based pan set over a gentle heat, melt together the butter, white chocolate and honey. Remove from the heat, then transfer one-third of the mixture to a small bowl and set aside to cool. Pour the remainder of the mixture, along with the coffee cream mixture, into a large mixing bowl.

Step two Place the shortbread in a plastic freezer bag and bash with a rolling pin until you have small pieces. Tip the shortbread pieces, mini marshmallows, macadamia nuts and fudge into the mixture in the large mixing bowl and mix well. Line a 23cm (9in) square brownie tin with clingfilm. Pour in the rocky road mixture and level off the surface. Pour on the reserved butter and white chocolate mixture and smooth the surface. Pop it into the fridge and leave to chill for at least 2 hours, or overnight.

Step three Lift the clingfilm up to take the biscuits out of the tin, and cut the rocky road into 24 squares to serve. They need to be kept chilled or they can become a bit sticky.

Makes 24 squares

100ml (4fl oz) double cream

1 tbsp instant espresso granules

125g (4½ oz) unsalted butter, softened

300g (10½ oz) white chocolate, broken into pieces

3 tbsp honey

200g (7oz) shortbread

100g (4oz) mini marshmallows

100g (4oz) macadamia nuts, toasted

100g (4oz) fudge, chopped into small cubes

Rosewater and Cardamom Crème Brûlée with Pistachios

You'll see that North African influences are strong in these aromatic little puds. The cardamom and rosewater complement the creamy custard, and the pistachio transforms this familiar dish.

Serves 4

570ml (18fl oz) double cream

5 cardamom pods

6 egg yolks

7 tbsp golden caster sugar

2 tbsp rosewater

1 tsp vanilla extract

2 tbsp shelled pistachio nuts, chopped, to serve

Step one In a small pan, heat the cream and cardamom really gently over a very low heat until tiny bubbles start to show around the edges, so that the cardamom infuses the cream with flavour. Meanwhile, in a bowl mix the egg yolks with 3 tablespoons of sugar. Remove the cardamom pods from the hot cream and then with a balloon whisk, whisk the cream really quickly into the sweetened egg mix until combined. Add the rosewater and vanilla extract and leave to infuse for 10 minutes. Meanwhile, preheat the oven to 140°C/275°F/gas 1.

Step two Divide the infused custard between 4 ramekins. Lay a piece of kitchen paper in the bottom of a roasting tray and place the ramekins in the tray. Boil the kettle and add enough boiling water to come halfway up the sides of the ramekins in the roasting tray. Place the tray on the lowest shelf of the oven and bake for 30 minutes, checking 5 minutes before they are due to be finished – you want them to be like a wobbly, loose jelly, as they will set more as they cool. If you cook them until they are fully set they will taste eggy and may even scramble a bit.

Step three Remove the ramekins from the roasting tray and leave to cool at room temperature for 30 minutes, then chill in the fridge for at least 2 hours, or overnight.

Step four When you're ready to serve the crème brûlées, dust the tops with the remaining 4 tablespoon of sugar. Using a cook's blowtorch or under a very hot grill, heat until the sugar has turned golden and caramelised. Give the topping a minute or two to set (this may take a little longer if done under the grill), then sprinkle with pistachios to serve.

Eton Mess with Passion Fruit, Lemon Curd and Raspberries

Eton mess has to be one of the most brilliant desserts ever. It's light, it has texture and it's super more-ish. Traditionally, it's served with berries, but I've given it a bit of a twist by using lemon curd and passion fruits too.

Step one Whisk together the double cream, icing sugar and vanilla extract until it becomes thick, but is still able to leave a trail. Don't over whip it and make it foamy as it will begin to taste a little buttery, or sometimes even cheesey!

Step two Add the broken-up meringues, lemon curd and raspberries to the mixture and give it all a good mix. The gentler you do it, the more obvious the marble effect of the lemon curd running through it will be. Divide among four plates, then top each plate with some of the passion fruit pulp.

Serves 4

300ml (½ pint) double cream

1 tbsp icing sugar

a few drops of vanilla extract

4 large ready-made meringues, broken up

5 tbsp good-quality ready-made lemon curd

150g (5 oz) fresh raspberries

2 passion fruits, pulped

Peach and Amaretto Tarts

Almond frangipane is the stuff that you get in the middle of an almond croissant – one of life's rather spectacular inventions. It goes well with a few fruits but I reckon peaches look fantastic and taste pretty damn good, too, and so work really well in these swanky little tarts. Serve them piping hot out of the oven with a hefty dollop of ice cream.

Serves 4

125g (4½ oz) ground almonds

100g (4oz) unsalted butter

1 egg

1 tbsp Amaretto liqueur (optional)

50g (2oz) icing sugar

300g (10½ oz) (roughly half a packet) all butter puff pasrty

3 ripe but firm peaches, halved, cored and sliced

vanilla ice cream, to serve

Step one Heat the oven to 200°C/425°F/gas 7. Beat the almonds, butter, egg, Amaretto (if using) and half the sugar in a small bowl until mixed.

Step two Roll the pastry out to the thickness of a 50p coin and, using a saucer about 13cm (5in) in diameter, cut out 4 circles. Lift the circles onto a baking sheet and spread each thinly with 2 tablespoons of almond mixture, leaving a border all around. Arrange the peach slices on top in a rosette and chill for at least 10 minutes.

Step three Bake for 25 minutes or until the pastry is crisp and the peach is sticky and caramelised. Serve with vanilla ice cream on the side.

10 9 8 7 6 5 4 3 2 1

Published in 2012 by Virgin Books, an imprint of Ebury Publishing. A Random House Group company.

Recipes © Gizzi Erskine 2012
Book design © Virgin Books 2012

All non-original recipes in this book first appeared in Gizzi Erskine's Kitchen Magic (2010) or on Gizzi Erskine's website www.gizzierskine.co.uk.

Gizzi Erskine has asserted her right to be identified as the author of this Work in accordance with the Copyright, Designs and Patents Act 1988

The Random House Group Limited
Reg. No. 954009

A CIP catalogue record for this book is available from the British Library

The Random House Group Limited supports The Forest Stewardship Council (FSC®), the leading international forest certification organisation. Our books carrying the FSC label are printed on FSC® certified paper. FSC is the only forest certification scheme endorsed by the leading environmental organisations, including Greenpeace. Our paper procurement policy can be found at www.randomhouse.co.uk/environment

Addresses for companies within the Random House Group can be found at www.randomhouse.co.uk

To buy books by your favourite authors and register for offers visit www.randomhouse.co.uk

Printed and bound in the UK by Butler, Tanner and Dennis Ltd
Colour origination by AltaImage

Commissioning Editor: Muna Reyal
Project Editor: Hannah Knowles
Editorial Assistant: Yvonne Jacob
Designer: Lucy Stephens
Food Stylist: Katie Giovanni
Prop Stylist: Wei Tang
Production: Rebecca Jones

Author photograph on page 4 © Chris Terry

Photography on pages 11, 14, 16, 18, 26, 29, 45, 49, 50, 58, 62, 69, 77, 89, 90, 98, 101, 102, 109, 117, 122, 125, 126, 129, 133, 137, 142, 145, 146, 153, 154, 176, 178, 181, 185, 186, 189, 190, 193, 194, 197, 198, 201 © David Loftus; Photography on pages 7, 9, 13, 20, 22, 25, 30, 32, 34, 37, 38, 41, 46, 53, 54, 57, 61, 65, 66, 70, 73, 74,.79, 81, 83, 93, 94, 97, 105, 106, 110, 113, 114, 118, 121, 130, 134, 138, 141, 149, 157, 158, 161, 162, 166, 169, 170 by William Reavell © Virgin Books 2012; Photography on pages 42, 85, 87, 172 174, 182, 202, 205 © Ian O'Leary; Photography on page 150 © Myles New; Photography on page 165 © Karen Thomas and British Lion Eggs www.eggrecipes.co.uk

ISBN: 9780753540589

MIX
Paper from responsible sources
FSC® C023561